Islamic Schools in France

Carine Bourget

Islamic Schools in France

Minority Integration and Separatism in Western Society

Carine Bourget
Department of French and Italian
University of Arizona
Tucson, AZ, USA

ISBN 978-3-030-03833-5   ISBN 978-3-030-03834-2 (eBook)
https://doi.org/10.1007/978-3-030-03834-2

Library of Congress Control Number: 2018962756

© The Editor(s) (if applicable) and The Author(s) 2019
This work is subject to copyright. All rights are solely and exclusively licensed by the Publisher, whether the whole or part of the material is concerned, specifically the rights of translation, reprinting, reuse of illustrations, recitation, broadcasting, reproduction on microfilms or in any other physical way, and transmission or information storage and retrieval, electronic adaptation, computer software, or by similar or dissimilar methodology now known or hereafter developed.
The use of general descriptive names, registered names, trademarks, service marks, etc. in this publication does not imply, even in the absence of a specific statement, that such names are exempt from the relevant protective laws and regulations and therefore free for general use.
The publisher, the authors and the editors are safe to assume that the advice and information in this book are believed to be true and accurate at the date of publication. Neither the publisher nor the authors or the editors give a warranty, express or implied, with respect to the material contained herein or for any errors or omissions that may have been made. The publisher remains neutral with regard to jurisdictional claims in published maps and institutional affiliations.

Cover illustration: Tom Howey, © Aysegul Muhcu/Alamy Stock Photo

This Palgrave Macmillan imprint is published by the registered company Springer Nature Switzerland AG
The registered company address is: Gewerbestrasse 11, 6330 Cham, Switzerland

A Averroès, Eva de Vitray, Al Kindi, MHS, La Plume, La Réussite et Samarcande,

Je tiens à exprimer ma gratitude la plus sincère à toutes les écoles qui m'ont chaleureusement ouvert leurs portes, tous ceux et celles qui ont pris le temps de me faire découvrir leur projet éducatif avec tant d'enthousiasme et de passion, et qui m'ont accueillie dans leurs classes. Ce livre n'aurait pu être écrit sans vous, il vous est dédié.

A ma famille, des deux côtés de l'Atlantique: Jacqueline, Daniel et Guillaume Martin; Marwan, Yasmine, Eyad et Zayd Krunz.

Acknowledgements

People who founded, work, and volunteer in the schools I visited have been vital to this project, which could not have been completed without them. I offer my sincere gratitude to the teams of Averroès, Eva de Vitray, Al Kindi, MHS, La Plume, La Réussite, and IFSQY/Samarcande for opening their doors, generously taking the time to explain their educational projects with enthusiasm and passion, and for welcoming me in their classes, often without any or much advance notice. I thank Youssef Aallam, Makhlouf Mamèche, Dhaou Meskine, Fatila Ould Saïd, Shakeel Siddiq, and the many others who have preferred to stay anonymous or simply did not have the time to answer my request for written permission to cite their names. Some of the people who make these schools run are stretched very thin, and I appreciate all the more the time they gave me. I also thank the Ministry of Education for granting me a very informative interview.

I am grateful to my colleagues and staff from the Department of French & Italian, The School of International Languages, Literatures, and Cultures, the College of Humanities, the School of Middle Eastern and North African Studies, and the Center for Middle Eastern Studies at the University of Arizona for providing an intellectually stimulating and supportive work environment, and to the following individuals in particular for their friendship and/or support over many years: Irène D'Almeida, Dalila Ayoun, Anne Betteridge, Beppe Cavatorta, Julia Clancy-Smith, Alain-Philippe Durand, Anne-Marie Engels-Brooks, Aileen Feng, Adel Gamal, Leila Hudson, Marie-Pierre Le Hir, Lise

Leibacher, Scott Lucas, Reg McGinnis, Maha Nassar; beyond Arizona: Safoi Babana-Hampton, Anne Donadey, Nouri Gana, Waïl Hassan, Valérie Orlando, Chantal Zabus; and beyond academia Ewa Alsbiei. I thank the College of Humanities for a Faculty Initiatives Grant that helped to defray the cost of travel for research in 2016. Special acknowledgements go to Marie-Pierre Le Hir for her detailed comments on some of the chapters, and to Eyad Krunz for proofreading the entire manuscript. Any errors and shortcomings are mine.

A very special note of gratitude is owed to my husband. This book could not have been written without his constant support, confidence, and encouragement, not to mention taking care of our busy household while I was away for field work. Many thanks to my children for stepping up while I was finishing the writing: to the older ones for helping with their little brother and to my youngest for taking it upon himself to prepare for dinner (the best over-easy eggs I've had!) when my deadline loomed.

Contents

Part I Background

1 *Communautarisme, Intégration*: The Terms of the Debate   3

2 Private Education Under Contract   19

Part II Introduction: Muslim Schools

3 Islamic Schools Successes: Averroes and Al-Kindi   55

4 Islamic Schools Challenges: Réussite and IFSQY/Samarcande   75

5 Islamic Schools Future: Elementary Education (La Plume, Eva de Vitray) and New Trends (MHS, Salafi, Clandestine, Non-contracted Schools by Choice, and Homeschooling)   99

6	**Arabic and Islamic Studies**	125
	Conclusion	153
	Index	171

List of Figures

Picture 3.1	Lycée Averroès, Lille, September 2016	56
Picture 3.2	Poster on the wall, Al-Kindi, Décines-Charpieu, September 2016	65
Picture 4.1	Mural in La Réussite's bathroom, Aubervilliers, March 2018	81
Picture 4.2	Students collages ("who is this?"), Samarcande, Montigny-le-Bretonneux, March 2018	94
Picture 4.3	A student poster, Samarcande	95
Picture 5.1	Eva de Vitray, Mantes-la-Jolie, September 2016	104
Picture 5.2	4th grade students' poster, Eva de Vitray	107

Introduction

The introduction lays out the background and motivation for the book, which proposes to answer the question as to whether Islam is compatible with the West through the study of private full-time Muslim education in France. This book is the first full-length study to analyze this growing phenomenon. I describe the climate in France where Islam has been the source of many domestic controversies since 1989, as well as terrorist attacks carried out by French Muslim citizens. I explain the choice of term used to label the schools under question (Muslim schools), and give an overview of the content of each chapter.

* * *

Is Islam compatible with the West? Recent events in France would prompt many people to answer a resounding no to this question. The year 2015 was a particularly devastating year that put the French Muslim community under the international spotlight: from the attacks on *Charlie Hebdo* in January 2015, to the ones by ISIS operatives on November 13, 2015 at the Stade de France, Bataclan, and restaurants that killed at least 130 and wounded over 300 people. These and other terrorist attacks in France and Europe are further exacerbating anti-Islam sentiments, given that some of the attackers were French citizens born and raised in France.

Controversial issues linked to the presence of Muslims in France have been making national headlines well before 2015. In France, the debate over the presence of Muslims in the nation started with the Muslim headscarf affair in 1989. The notorious "affaire du foulard," 'affair of the [Muslim] scarf,'[1] sparked in 1989 when three teenage girls were expelled from their public middle school for refusing to remove their headscarves, received much coverage from the media. Similar incidents reoccurred over the years and culminated into the 2004 law that bans certain religious signs in public schools. Although the debate on the issue of the scarf was framed by secularism, with concerns over gender equality adding fuel to the fire, several scholars have pointed out that what was really at stake was the issue of immigration, and more specifically, the realization that a population that was considered foreign and composed of temporary immigrants had actually settled down and was there to stay. As Michel Wieviorka pointed out, "the various forms of Islam in France have more to do with issues in French society than with issues from the originating societies" (101).

In the second half of the twentieth century, metropolitan France has become home to a substantial Muslim minority, composed mostly of immigrant Maghrebian workers and their descendants. In less than half a century, Islam has climbed to be the second religion of France, mostly through immigration from North Africa. The fact that this population comes from former French colonies plays a major factor, as colonial baggage and stereotypes about Islam contribute to skewing the debate. Because immigrants were for the most part confined to the outskirts of French society, they remained invisible until the 1980s.

As Thomas Deltombe has shown in his extensive analysis of coverage on French TV from 1975 to 2004, Islam in France was often scrutinized through the prism of foreign events (9). The heated domestic debate about the issue of the veil in public schools took place in a context in which Islam was associated with distressing national and international headlines in the 1990s, such as the Algerian civil war and the Taliban in Afghanistan. The issue of the veil in public schools became the symbol of what were seen as both internal and external threats to France, and its prohibition as an expedient to solve social problems of Islamism, sexism, and violence in the suburbs. The intensifying determination of successive governments to address the Muslim question—symbolically, by taking a firm stand on headscarves—came in reaction to the growing popularity and electoral success of Jean-Marie Le Pen's Far Right National Front party.

The law banning the headscarf in public schools was followed by the law banning the face covering in public. The Muslim veil in various forms has become a decried symbol of Islamic fundamentalism, ethnic separatism or *communitarisme*, and sexism, none of which are compatible with the secular French Republic that claims equality for all its citizens in a nation constructed as one and indivisible.

This book was sparked by research for a chapter on the French Muslim headscarf affair in my last book. Significantly, the debate on religious signs in public schools was triggered by the presence of a Muslim sign in a place that is supposed to be the gateway to integration, namely the public school. As I pointed out in that chapter, one consequence of the affair is that it will have, ironically given that the debate was framed around the issue of secularism, spurred the establishment of private Islamic schools that would eventually receive government subsidies. A handful of these Muslim schools are now receiving government funds, like most of their Jewish and Catholic counterparts.

This book is the first to analyze the growing phenomenon of private full-time Muslim education in France. From a conference talk given in 2013, this project has expanded into a book to reflect the exponential development of Muslim schools and projects for new schools in France. When I started this research in 2013, there were no publications other than newspaper articles and one part in a report commissioned by the Interior Ministry in 2010. A team of researchers was charged with doing a survey of the teaching of Islam in three structures, including private Muslim schools but also Qur'anic schools and Higher education Islamic institutes (Bras et al.). That report puts the development of private Muslim schools in relation with three factors: the Muslim Brothers activism through the UOIF trying to promote "a Muslim citizenship" "une citoyenneté musulmane", the crisis of public schools, and the 2004 law against the headscarf. They counted ten schools at the time, half of them affiliated with the UOIF. This report states that Muslim schools present "a reassuring window/showcase" (74), with an emphasis on the national curriculum, academic excellence, and Islam. But it talks about three schools only and tends to overgeneralize some features. Moreover, it is not particularly conclusive: on the one hand, pointing out that the religious aspect of the schools are second to academic excellence and that Islam is a means to citizenship and integration (Bras et al. 74), but ending by wondering whether the "Muslim citizenship" preached by the UOIF is compatible with the French Republic citizenship (Bras et al. 75).

Since then, Muslim schools have drawn further attention, but only a few scholarly articles have appeared so far.[2] A call from the government to researchers specific to Muslim schools in 2015 went unanswered; it was reissued in 2016 for research to be conducted in 2017.[3] The funding of this research project dedicated to Muslim schools in France by the French government[4] might indicate a shift. In my second visit in 2018, others names were mentioned,[5] so I expect additional research to be available soon.

Regardless of their exact number, this study investigates whether Islamic schools participate in the much-condemned *communautarisme* (or ethnic/cultural separatism) that the Muslim community is often accused of, or whether their founding is a sign of *intégration* (or assimilation) into the French Republic, given that most of private education in France is subsidized by the government. As John Bowen noted in his seminal chapter on La Réussite, "is the phrase 'Islamic Republican school' an oxymoron?" (110). When he conducted his study, there were only a few "Muslim private day schools," as he chose to call them (110). Bowen dedicated a chapter on La Réussite and its founder, Dhaou Meskine, because of the range of activities he leads to create "Muslim-ambiance institutions," including a school, an institute, a summer camp, and a network of imams (110). Indeed, Bowen points out that, on the one hand, these schools "signal the integration of Muslims into the State system," along with Catholic and Jewish schools, and that some in government see it as an outlet for Muslim communalist sentiments to be kept out of the public schools (116). On the other hand, such schools minimize students' contacts with non-Muslims and might impede "integration" (Bowen 116). This study adds to our understanding of the so-called resurgence of religion following the demise of the secularization theory, brings new understanding on the place of religion in the West, and of Islam in diasporic contexts, and sheds new light on how Muslim minorities adapt and evolve.

Islamic or Muslim Schools?

To understand and analyze the growing phenomenon of Muslim schools in France, I must explain the choice of terms used to label the schools under question: are they Islamic schools or Muslim schools? My original title, "Communautarisme or Intégration? Muslim Schools in France," did not meet approval from the marketing department, who expressed a preference for a more straightforward title, to help ensure that scholars and students would quickly find the book in relevant subject/word search in libraries as well as on sites like Barnes & Noble and Amazon. We compromised on the present title, *Islamic Schools in France*, even though throughout the book I refer to these schools as Muslim and not Islamic.

Larousse, the most common dictionary, does not differentiate much between the two terms, with the adjectives "islamique" "Islamic" defined as "relatif à l'islam" "relating to Islam" and "musulman" "Muslim" as "relatif à l'islam, se dit d'un fidèle de l'islam" "relating to Islam, said about followers of Islam" (Larousse.fr). Many people use them as equivalent (see, for example, Alain Gresh's editorial), though "Muslim" is wider than Islamic since it encompasses both things related to the faith and the people who follow it.

Ahmed Souaiaia argues that even though scholars use them interchangeably, there is a subtle distinction and they are not completely identical. Taking the example of architecture, he explains that:

> The phrase *Islamic architecture* refers to architecture that is broadly influenced, limited, inspired, informed by Islamic values, even if it is produced by non-Muslim persons. *Islamic architecture* might consist of purely Islam-inspired elements, but it might also consist of elements that are not inspired and influenced by Islam or Muslim architects. By contrast, the term *Muslim architecture* is attributive, not descriptive. It refers to architecture created by Muslim persons. Where *Islamic architecture* is a broad descriptive term, accurate use of the term *Muslim architecture* requires a specific context (1).
>
> With this distinction in mind, it becomes clear that the adjective *Muslim* is exclusive whereas the adjective *Islamic* is inclusive. Not all Islamic things are produced by Muslims, but Muslim-produced things must be things produced by individuals who are Muslim.

Based on this definition and nuances between the two, the schools in this book are Muslim schools in the sense that they have all been founded by Muslim people. However, whether one can say that they are Islamic is highly debatable. None of the schools identified themselves in French as "islamique," always as "musulmane". The difference between the two reflects that Islam is not the main *raison d'être* for these schools.

Contents

The book is divided into two parts. Part I lays the foundation by giving background information about the context in which the schools emerged, focusing on the history of Islam in France and the history of religious private education, specifically French debates and conflicts over Catholic and Republican schools.

Chapter 1: *Communautarisme, Intégration*: The Terms of the Debate examines the two terms that are at the heart of the debate about Muslims' assimilation in French society: *communautarisme* and *intégration*. In the French context, *communautarisme* carries a negative connotation, because it is deemed as incompatible with the values of universalism promoted by the French model of the nation. On the other hand, *intégration* is the goal that the nation fosters for all immigrants and their descendants, but one that Muslim minorities who claim their identity are faulted for eluding. Elements of this debate have been playing out on public schools grounds through cases such as the headscarf affair, the issue of halal meat in school cafeterias, and others. I recapitulate findings that show the diversity and the integration of the majority of Muslims in France, and the discrimination and accusations of double talk they face.

Chapter 2: Private Education Under Contract summarizes the contemporary history of private education in France and various debates and controversies surrounding government education subsidies, which started in the second half of the twentieth century. It surveys issues related to private education in France since the 1905 law of separation of Church and State, and especially after WWII, detailing what is known as the "school war" or "guerre scolaire" between public and private education. These battles took place between proponents of the public system and defenders of private (religious) education, the latter still overwhelmingly catholic, and well before Islam's presence was felt in metropolitan France. It explains the contract that private religious schools can sign with the French government to obtain public funding. With the 1959 Debré law, private schools are eligible for substantial subsidies from the State, provided that the school teaches the nationally mandated curriculum, accepts all teachers, and does not make religious instruction mandatory. This chapter insists on the politics involved around the Debré law which provides for government subsidies, and the failed attempt to repeal that law in 1984 because of public outcry. About 17% of pupils in France attend 8800 private schools; 98% of these students attend a school under contract with the state. According to statistics published in 2008, 8000 Catholic schools were teaching 2 million children, 256 Jewish schools teaching 30,000 children, and 5 Muslim schools teaching 600 children. Although the Muslim population in France is estimated to be 3–6% of the population, only four Muslim schools have succeeded to date in getting funding by the State. This chapter explains some of the reasons why Muslim schools are lagging behind other faith-based schools, including difficulties linked to the process for getting state funding and the demographics of the Muslim population. It also discusses briefly the evolution of other minority faith-based schools (Jewish and Protestant) in order to compare and situate the creation of Muslim schools.

Part II draws mostly on field work, during which I examined materials used in classrooms, observed Arabic and Islamic education classes, and spoke with school administrators and teachers at schools in 2016 (Averroès, Al Kindi, Eva de Vitray and La Plume) and in 2018 (IFSQY/Samarcande, MHS, Réussite, Eva de Vitray). The introduction to the second part of the book gives numbers and statistics about the growth of Muslim schools in France, and a summary of reactions to that growth. It then explains how field work was conducted in Fall 2016 and Spring 2018, during which I examined materials used in classrooms, observed Arabic and Islamic education classes, and spoke with school administrators and teachers. For the most part, the schools were selected because they were pioneers: the first elementary school, the first middle school, the first school to get a contract with the state, etc. This is detailed in each section. I also tried unsuccessfully to visit several schools in the Seine-St-Denis department.

The chapters that focus on the schools (Chapters 3–6) give an overview of the history and of the stated goals and mission of each school on their website, many of which make it a top priority to help students reconcile their identity as Muslim French. It then examines how the schools' objectives translate into practice, focusing on how school administrators and teachers endeavor to achieve those goals. I examine how religious education is both similar to and different from the traditional religious instruction offered in majority-Muslim countries.

Chapter 3: Islamic Schools Successes: Averroes and Al Kindi is divided into two parts. Averroes and Al Kindi are two major players in the landscape of private Muslim schools in France. Despite having faced controversies, both have weathered them without affecting their contract with the State. Part I of this chapter details the history of the first Islamic school to succeed in signing a contract with the state from its founding through its recent success. Averroes High School made national headlines in 2013 after being ranked the best high school in France. It has also made negative headlines, when a former teacher accused the school of various offenses it was eventually cleared of. Part II focuses on Al Kindi, which at some point was the largest Muslim school in France, and the first to range from K-12.[6]

Chapter 4: Islamic Schools Challenges: Réussite and IFSQY/ Samarcande focuses on two schools that illustrate some of the difficulties encountered by Muslim schools to get a contract with the State. The first part focuses on the first private junior high Muslim school, opened in October 2001 by the association Réussite. This association had been doing after-school tutoring for 9 years prior to the opening of a full-time school. One of the goals of the association Réussite is to fight school failure in the department of Seine-St-Denis, which has been traditionally working class and notorious for its failed housing policies that have created ghettos. The Réussite School submitted all paperwork to the State and underwent an inspection in June 2006 as part of the contract application. Despite impressive results at national exams in 2008, the school waited for an answer from the state for eight years, only to have its request denied in 2014. In the meantime, debts accumulated and the school had to first close some of its classes before shutting down completely in 2017. The second school, known as IFSQY or Samarcande, was denied its first request for a contract for lack of funding.

Chapter 5: Islamic Schools Future: Elementary Education and New Trends (MHS, Salafi, Clandestine, Non-contracted Schools by Choice, and Homeschooling) is divided into two parts. Part I investigates the recent trend of opening elementary rather than secondary schools. It focuses on two primary schools: La Plume in Grenoble, the first Muslim elementary school in France, and Eva-de-Vitray in Mantes-la-Jolie, the first Muslim elementary school in metropolitan France to get a contract with the state. The second part discusses schools at both ends of the spectrum: a secular school with Muslim ethics (MHS), a school reported to be Salafi, clandestine schools, a school that might not want a contract with the State, and homeschooling. Only the first one granted me access; I describe what I learned during unsuccessful attempts at visiting the others.

Chapter 6: Arabic and Islamic Studies is divided into two parts. Part I raises the issue of the toll that obvious and pernicious exclusion of Muslim students' culture (such as the exclusion of Islamic practices in public schools and the absence and/or slanted view of Muslim students' culture in the curriculum) can take on parents and students. Part II examines the curriculum used by each school for the subjects not offered in public schools, namely Arabic[7] and Islamic studies. During field work conducted in 2016 and 2018, I examined materials used and conducted class observations for these subjects. I look at how the traditional field of Islamic education has been adapted to build both national and religious identities among French Muslim students, and how these classes participate in the making of a French Islam.

Conclusion recapitulates the findings of this study: that Muslim schools debunk culturalist arguments about the exceptional and fundamental impossibility of Muslim communities to integrate in Western societies because of their religious beliefs and practice. It sums up findings that show the diversity of Muslim schools despite many commonalities, their existence as a sign of integration, and looks at future challenges related to federating these schools, gender issues, and finding acceptance in French society at large.

Notes

1. In France, the incident was referred to as "l'affaire du foulard" 'the affair of the scarf.' I use the terms scarf and veil interchangeably, as was done in France, to refer to a head cover only, and face veil for something that hides the face.
2. When I did field work in 2016, Al Kindi and Averroes mentioned Carole Ferrara, whose article just came out (2018). Al-Kindi also mentioned hosting a group of Japanese researchers and Australians from the Commonwealth.
3. « Etablissements scolaires musulmans en France : un état des lieux » (Projet n°10-2016) was attributed to Rania Hanafi and Jean-François Bruneaud (Univ. Nice Sophia Antipolis). I contacted them in Spring 2018 as I was finishing this manuscript, but they were still writing out their report. In a personal email from the person responsible at the Bureau central des cultes, I was informed that the project was due in Summer 2018 with planned publication via Openédition/La Documentation française.

4. A partnership between the Ministry of Education and the Ministry of Interior, the latter houses the Bureau Central des Cultes in charge of organized religions.
5. Another was a student from the Ecole Pratique des Hautes Etudes Ivry.
6. K-12 is a misnomer in the French context where elementary school starts with first grade and lasts five years as opposed to six in the US. Kindergarten in France corresponds to the last year of preschool. However, in this study, I use the term K-12 common in the US as a shortcut to designate primary and secondary education.
7. Arabic is offered in a few public schools as a foreign language.

References

Bowen, John. *Can Islam Be French? Pluralism and Pragmatism in a Secularist State.* Princeton: Princeton University Press, 2009.

Bras, J.-P., S. Mervin, S. Amghar, L. Fournier, O. Marongiu, and B. Godard. "L'enseignement de l'Islam dans les écoles coraniques, les institutions de formation islamique et les écoles privées." Rapport du IISMM & EHESS, 2010. http://www.disons.fr/wp-content/uploads/2012/03/RAPPORTENSEIGNEMENT-ISLAMIQUE-final.pdf.

Deltombe, Thomas. *L'Islam imaginaire : la construction médiatique de l'islamophobie en France, 1975–2005.* Paris: La Découverte, 2005.

Ferrara, Carol. "Transmitting Faith in the Republic: Muslim Schooling in Modern Plural France." *Religious Education* 113.1 (2018): 14–25.

Gresh, Alain. « Pour en finir avec l'adjectif « musulman » (ou « islamique »). » *Le Monde diplomatique*, 3 August 2012. https://blog.mondediplo.net/2012-08-03-Pour-en-finir-avec-l-adjectif-musulman-ou.

Souaiaia, Ahmed E. "What Is The Difference Between 'Muslim' And 'Islamic'?" *Islamic Societies Review*, 6 November 2016: 1–3. http://www.reasonedcomments.org/2016/11/what-is-difference-between-muslim-and.html.

Wieviorka, Michel. "Race, Culture, and Society: The French Experience with Muslims." *Muslim Europe or Euro-Islam: Politics, Culture and Citizenship in the Age of Globalization.* Ed. Nezar Alsayyad and Manuel Castelles. New York: Lexington Books, 2002. 100–109.

Zwilling, Anne-Laure. "France." *Yearbook of Muslims in Europe 8.* Ed. Oliver Scharbrodt, Samim Akgönül, Ahmet Alibašić, Jørgen Nielsen, and Egdunas Račius. Leiden: Brill, 254–284.

PART I

Background

CHAPTER 1

Communautarisme, Intégration: The Terms of the Debate

From Arabs to Muslims

As Mayanthi Fernando stated, Muslim French are "an object of serious consternation in France, and therefore a common object of study for French sociologists, anthropologists, and political scientists as well as a common target of governmental intervention" (26). Many of those studies have been policy-driven, and even when not, Muslims are "a problem to be solved" despite what many of them claim as their "right to indifference," as one of Fernando's interlocutors put it (26–27). Studies abound about the contemporary presence of Islam in France, some more historical or sociological, or a mix of both, as well as comparative studies about Islam in the West and/or Europe (see among many others Césari, Kepel, Davidson, Fetzer and Sedgwick, Fetzer and Soper, and Thomas). In general discourse, Islam "is either portrayed as a foreign culture, defined essentially by 'Arab' or 'Muslim' values as purportedly propagated by North African immigrants; or as a religion, often a fundamentalist one; or as a geopolitical force, in reference to the crises in the Middle East, the umma, and Islamist terrorism" (Laurence and Vaïsse ix). Three figures have emerged successively to characterize this segment of the population: first the "Arab immigrant" in the 1970s, followed by the "civic Beur" in the 1980s, and lastly, the "Muslim citizen" starting in 1989 (Laurence and Vaïsse 7).

Whether it refers to the culture or the religion, the connotation is always that Islam is foreign to France, and some aspects linked to its practice have generated intense debates, from the Muslim headscarf affair in 1989 to the burkini ban in 2016. Jonathan Laurence notes that the general climate in France and Europe does not seem to reflect the optimism of his 2012 title *Integrating Islam*, given a "succession of official restrictions on the outward expression of Muslim piety," including the French ban on burqas and the Italian discussion of a moratorium on building mosques following the Swiss ban on minarets among other things (1).

The question of the definition of who is Muslim is a fraught one. Leyla Arslan points out the difficulty of first of all defining and then counting Muslims: "Sociological Muslims (whatever relations they have with religion) born in Muslim families probably number between 4 and 5 million [...]. Using this methodology, Muslims are individuals and their descendants from Muslim countries such as North Africa, Turkey, Sub-Saharan Africa and Pakistan. The children of the second generation and converts are excluded from this figure" (189). This definition is problematic and exclusive. Fredette considers that being Muslim in France can be a religious or a cultural affiliation (8), while Sharif Gemie is more encompassing and uses the term Muslim to refer to "at once a faith, a culture, and a status" (12). Traditional estimates range from 2 million practicing Muslims to 6 million if one adds cultural Muslims. Regardless of whether Muslims are believers, cultural, or ethnic Muslims, they have been increasingly accused of *communautarisme*.

Communautarisme

Communautarisme is a difficult term to translate into English, because it does not carry the same baggage in French as in English. *Communautarisme* implies valuing an affiliation to an ethnic/religious community above integration to the collective, and thus threatens the unity of the Nation. As Gemie notes, "France is probably the only country in the world in which a word linked to the term 'community' carries severely negative connotations. 'Communautarisme' does not mean an innocent activity to build up a community: instead, it means a challenge to the Republican ideal of a transparent, unified public sphere in which all citizens appear as approximate equals" (Gemie 15). The notion of appearances is crucial here, as many controversies in France tend to deal with issues related to religious visibility of Muslims rather than issues of inequalities. *Communautarisme* has been translated by various terms, including communalism (Bowen 2007; Tolan 47), communitarianism (Roy), ethnic separatism or factionalism (Begag xviii), and ghettoization understood as a move initiated by an ethnic or cultural minority group to retreat from a common secular public domain (Gemie 15; Mazawi 235–236). I choose to retain the term in its original French to encompass all these definitions and keep negative connotations.

Fabrice Dhume-Sonzogni's survey shows that the term *communautarisme* is very recent in the press; it started appearing in 1995 and was listed in a dictionary for the first time in 1997 (24–25). It is often linked to multiculturalism, associated with an Anglo-Saxon counter-model that should be rejected (25). Dhume-Sonzogni shows that *communautarisme* is the mark of the dominant, who labels his legitimate view of the world as 'universalism' and consequently labels what does not fit into it as an illegitimate '*communautarisme*' (31). The anti-*communautarisme* discourse is paradoxically the only one that talks about *communautarisme*; it is therefore less an actual social phenomenon than a manifestation of the fantasy about the Other that is always defined by its supposed origin (Dhume-Sonzogni 34–35). *Communautarisme* is commonly associated with a *repli* or withdrawal into self-segregation or protests and demands for specific rights (Tissot).

The concept, if not the term itself, of *communautarisme* has been used for other minorities in modern France. Elmaleh notes that French society broke with the Jacobine tradition for the first time by recognizing officially the idea of a Jewish community (569). When Elmaleh remarks that WWII first slowed down, then accelerated the process of founding Jewish schools in France that started in the 1920s, he states that he cannot use the term *communautarisme* to characterize this process because it would be anachronistic to do so, so he names it a "collective awareness of being Jewish in France" "prise de conscience collective de l'être-juif en France" (140), and notes that it will be attributed to Muslims later on (569).

Scholars have noted that in contemporary France, *communautarisme*, a term that has been increasingly used in politics to stir up ideological electoral gains, always connotes a threat that is posed by Islam (Dhume-Sonzogni 48). As Gérard Noiriel points out in a book that analyzes the use of the concept of national identity during the 2007 presidential campaign, there is no need to explain what *communautarisme* means because everybody knows it refers to Muslims (*L'identité nationale* 94). Gemie tells a joke that shows the double standards that are applied to Muslims only among many other groups in France: "When a group of

Bretons meet in the street, it's called regionalism; when it's a group of Portuguese, it's called folklore; and when it's a group of North Africans, it's called communautarisme" (15). Muslims are the only group widely seen as partaking in *communautarisme* through various specific demands and a perceived refusal to integrate; they are the regular target of controversies fueled by the media and politicians (Seniguer).

In an analysis of a report by the Secret Services published in 2004, Tissot examines how designating socioeconomic and racial segregation under the term *communautarisme* hides the real causes of various failed State policies (lodging, schooling) while putting the blame on the people who are suffering the consequences of those policies. She concludes that there is an inversion of causes and effects: *communautarisme* is not seen as a consequence of various discriminations, but as the cause of all problems. *Communautarisme* is thus constructed as the reason for the failure of integration, and not as a consequence or reaction to it (Dhume-Sonzogni 148). Commenting on the criteria that were used for the report,[1] Dhume-Sonzogni notes that visibility is seen as a sign of *repli* (withdrawal) (49–50), and concludes that brandishing the theme of *communautarisme* functions as a self-fulfilling prophecy (51). Moreover, several scholars have argued that there has been a "racialization of the category of 'Muslims'" (Talpin et al. 28, Tevanian, Keaton), which has led Pierre Tevanian to write that the word *communautarisme* has become a "métaphore du racisme respectable" 'metaphor for respectable racism,' in other words, a way to designate a racialized group without having to name Arabs, Blacks, and/or Muslims (cited in Tissot).

Exaggerations and hyperboles played out during the headscarf affair and resurfaced during various controversies. Scholars have noted the disproportionate measures of passing laws or local ordinances to address practices that concerned minuscule numbers. Some of the language used in the campaign for the anti-face covering law is an example of such excess. Regarding the law about face covering in public spaces, Joppke and Torpey note "the disproportionate measure of passing a law to reign in an ultramarginal practice by less than one-tenth of a percent of France's Muslim population" and that "If one of the main instigators of the burqa campaign, André Gerin, ignoring the tiny numbers laid out to his commission by no less than the interior minister himself, deemed French society in the grip of 'Talibanization' and drowning in a 'marée noire' (oil slick) of dark Muslim veils, this was moral panic, better understood in psycho-pathological than politicorational terms" (22).

Yet, when laws whose impetus are Muslim signs are passed, they are always phrased in terms that do not single out nor even refer to Muslims, in line with the French ideal of universalism. However, nobody is duped: as Fredette notes, "elite challenges to Muslim citizenship are primarily discursive, and where laws have a disparate impact on Muslims, they are facially neutral and do not single out Muslims in their texts" (Fredette 6). But everybody knew that the 2004 law was spurred by a Muslim sign, just as everybody knows that Muslims are the target when there are talks about passing a new law to ban prayers in the streets, since they are the one religious group that suffers from lack of sufficient worshipping space and have made headlines for having worshippers spilling out into the street during service in some places.

Diversity of "the" French Muslim Community

Despite the construction in the media of Muslims as a unified block making demands for specific accommodations and being visible in the public space, research has consistently shown that "a striking gap exists between the image of Islam as it is constructed in binary public discourse and the multifaceted reality of Muslims across countries and localities" (Césari xiv). As Olivier Roy sarcastically points out, "if a Muslim community really existed, it would not have taken the government fifteen years to create a representative body for the Muslims of France, which would disintegrate in one day without the state's backing" (85).

Most scholars who have done extensive field work insist on the diversity of French Muslims. Laurence and Vaïsse argue that "a 'French Islam' is increasingly replacing the 'Islam in France' that has developed over the last thirty to forty years" (4). Their data and analysis emphasize the diversity of Muslims in France and a dynamic Muslim civil society (5). French Muslims constitute a very disparate community, split by national origin, ethnicity, and religious piety and practice (8). Brouard and Tiberj's study corroborates the same conclusion: "Finally, the New French cannot be characterized as a homogeneous group any more than the rest of the French can, contrary to what the very notion of *communautarisme* presupposes. The disputes over values (racism, authoritarianism, anti-Semitism, sexual intolerance, etc.) that cross French society as a whole do not spare the New French among them. From this point of view, they still seem French like the other French, like everyone else. Their diversity trumps their unity" (135). In his book, Olivier Roy titles a chapter "The Fantasy of Communitarianism" to debunk the fact that communautarianism at the levels of the banlieue (neighborhood) and umma (global and supranational) is actually a threat. According to him, it is at best a virtual phenomenon "which exists only in the imagination or on the Internet" (84). He insists that "there is no Muslim community in France but a scattered, heterogeneous population not very concerned with unifying itself or even with being really represented… The Muslim community has even less substance than the Jewish community in France; there are rather very diversified populations, only one segment of which agrees to recognize itself as primarily a religious community" (Roy 84).

Despite this recognition from researchers that there is no "one French Muslim identity," French elites consistently ignore this and manipulate this fabricated image of the Muslim as a threat to France and French identity. Fredette insists that "This points to an important aspect of elite power: the power to create identities and to judge those identities as deserving or undeserving of citizenship" (5). She also accentuates the disconnect between this general discourse conveyed by the media, politicians, and intellectuals, which portrays Muslims as a homogeneous group concerned first and foremost with religion, while Muslims see themselves as French citizens with several belongings that they do not see as incompatible (Fredette 8). This diversity is also reflected in the "extreme diversity of mobilisations of Muslims" (Talpin et al. 58). Talpin et al. underline that society is made up of communities, and that there are double standards as to which communities are looked down upon: as an example, they mention the areas where upper classes live as being the most homogenous socially and religiously, yet they are never labelled as *communautaristes* (24–25).

INTEGRATION

Not only are Muslims diverse, they do not see a conflict between their French and their Muslim identities. While general discourse implies that French Muslim is an oxymoron, several studies show that "On the whole, transnational religious and minority identifications are not alternatives to identification with France. They do not loosen ties to national identity. The religious dimension in particular is completely independent from that of identification with France. Religious, transnational, minority, and local identification are articulated alongside a national identification rather than opposing it" (Brouard and Tiberj 104–105). Similarly, the French Muslims interviewed by Fredette "spoke to the multiplicity and fluidity of their identities (or affiliations for those who deny that religion can be an identity). While they sometimes articulated different ways to balance being French and being Muslim, not one believed that those two memberships come into conflict" (169). Mayanthi Fernando chose to refer to her interlocutors as Muslim French, a term meant to translate the longer self-description that she heard most often: "citoyen français de confession musulmane" (French citizen of Muslim faith) (15). In this self-description, the French citizenship is the part that comes first.

Data collected by Laurence and Vaïsse show that intermarriage and the use of French at home, which are considered indicators of cultural integration have quickly risen over time, and that "the information presented on controversial issues like fertility rates and patterns of religious observance suggests a less alarming scenario than those often portrayed in the media" (8). But as Begag pointed out, the people who are integrated are invisible because their behavior is too ordinary to be of any interest to the media (47).

Assimilation

Dhume-Sonzogni insists that there is a logic of assimilation hiding behind the discourse on integration, and that the insistence on the fact that Muslims are never sufficiently integrated only further stigmatizes this group, which in turn justifies discrimination (152). Although he does not elaborate on the issue of assimilation, it is a recurring feature in various testimonies collected by Keaton (among others): that what the media and politicians mean by integration has more to do with the colonial ideology of assimilation. In her analysis of the four figures that dominated the French imaginary, Nacira Guénif-Souilamas points out the French Republic's inability to question itself; instead it projects its refusal to change and adapt onto an invented identity crisis from postcolonial immigrants and their descendants (129). She underlines the blind spot of this flawed integration concept: that Muslims should soften what makes them Muslims but not totally erase it so they can be recognized as such while being less threatening (128). While the landscape has changed and the terminology that describes the veiled girl, the Arab male youth (both negative), and their positive counterparts, that is the secular Muslim and the Beurette, should be updated, Guénif-Souilamas' basic framework still holds.

Tissot has also underlined that any reference to what is perceived as the country of origin by immigrants and their descendants is considered as a proof of lack of integration by a postcolonial assimilationist ideology, particularly when it comes to visible manifestations. But not all visible manifestations are given equal treatment. It is not so much that some Muslims are not just believing Muslims but practicing Muslims, but the fact that some of those practices are visible in the public space that concerns secularist die-hards in France. Thus, opposition to building mosques should be seen in this light: a mosque and its minaret are not part of the typical geographical landscape; praying inside a mosque is tolerated but not when it happens in the streets, etc. But from the Muslim French's point of view, as Fernando emphasizes, there is no contradiction between "democratic citizenship and public religiosity" (13).

Discrimination

Despite this integration, the future will unlikely be rosy, first of all because of the level of Islamophobia. A French journalist recently wrote: "I am a little Islamophobe" without much notice. As Gresh pointed out, it would be unimaginable that an editorial stating "I am a little Judeophobe" would be published. Laurence and Vaïsse's study also makes it clear that Muslims are lagging behind in terms of educational achievements and employment rates, and that discrimination, Islamophobia, and racism have led some French Muslims to feel bitter and resentful (8). Indeed, they surmise that it will be impossible to eradicate "disgruntled young radicals, bearded Islamists, racist behavior, and social ills of all sorts— images that may, to some extent or another, always be part of the picture of Islam in Europe" (Laurence and Vaïsse 4). Focusing on the children of immigrants or second generation who have achieved middle-class status, Jean Beaman "examine[s] how a population that is legally and technically French is not considered culturally French, and is therefore excluded from popular imaginations of who a French person is. This reveals how race, ethnicity, and culture intersect in determining who is a citizen of the nation-state and who can claim a French identity" (4). She demonstrates through field work that even though many children of North African immigrants are assimilated (that is, they have been educated at French schools and universities, their native language is French, and they are French citizens), they are still experiencing exclusion and discrimination (4). Many teachers and administrators I met during my visits have said that in the current climate in France, Muslims feel constantly on the defensive and are called out in the streets and public transportation, especially women, and blame politicians for islamizing the debate.

In his history of immigration in France, Noiriel points out that the decisive factor in previous waves of immigrants' assimilation was the work environment, and that this is what is missing in France with the high national unemployment rate (which is even much higher in underprivileged neighborhoods) and temporary employment (*Creuset* 355–356), especially for youth. A controlled study conducted by Claire Adida, David Laitin, and Marie-Anne Valfort demonstrates that Muslims experience significant discrimination in France, and that there is evidence that "Muslims, perceiving more hostility in France, separate more from the host society than do their Christian counterparts" (124).

In any case, Brouard and Tiberj's study shows that *communautarisme* "concerns only an extreme fringe minority of the New French" in France today and that it is "less a danger than a fantasy" (131). Indeed, they estimate that the group that exhibits *communautarisme*, defined as "presenting signs of disengagement from France as well as identification with religion and extranational solidarity" represents only 8 percent of their sample, a small minority (131). Talpin et al.'s collection of articles shows that Muslims' engagements that are studied in their volume is more about claiming equality than having their differences acknowledged (26).

Despite the French State's highly centralized bureaucracy, its many levels do lend room for disguised discrimination to happen against Muslim schools. For instance, because the opening of a school requires approval of various local authorities, the process lends itself to inconsistencies regarding approval due to mayors' preconceived ideas more than the quality of the project. As explained in one article, the same project was first rejected by the town of Bagnolet before being approved in neighboring Bobigny (Le Guellec). In another case, the Academy had opposed the opening of Eduk Ludik on the ground that the school was already operating like a school without having declared it, but the tribunal ruled that the only reasons to oppose the opening of a school should relate to good morals and hygiene (Beyer).

The State and Religions

The French state has been invoking the principle of secularism beginning with the headscarf affair as if it was a concept that was clearly defined and understood, but if anything else, the way events unfolded showed that the very concept of secularism is open to differing interpretations. Inconsistencies have been there all along, and one of the most obvious ones is the Concordat still in effect in Alsace-Moselle, but as long as Islam is not involved, breaches of secularism do not make headlines nor elicit heated debates and reactions. While some scholars think that there is an "ongoing process of mutual adaptation on the part of the French state and Muslims in France" (Laurence and Vaïsse 5), others point out that the French State never puts itself nor its claim of universalism into question and projects all the blame on Muslims for failing to integrate (Fredette 172). In fact, Fernando's study and others have shown that there are "long-standing tensions and contradictions immanent to laïcité and to republican citizenship, tensions not so much generated as precipitated by the presence of Muslim French." Her study shows the process by which, paradoxically, these tensions inherent in France's version of secularism are projected onto France's Muslims, who are then blamed for the State's very own inconsistencies, and not deemed worthy citizens (Fernando 6).

On another aspect, the French state has consistently followed the same approach toward religions: to have a representative to turn to when needed. Thanks to Catholicism's own hierarchy, the State has not had to intervene, as it has in the case of other religions. Napoleon founded the Consistory to represent Jews, and the rector of Paris' Great mosque was taken by the State by default as representing Muslims. That legitimacy was strongly put into question in the 1990s by many Muslims who did not feel represented by Paris' Great mosque, so the state launched a process that led after more than ten years to the creation of the Conseil Français du Culte Musulman (CFCM) in 2003 (Tolan 48–49). Following its Catholic, Protestant, and Jewish counterparts, its role is, among other things, to represent worship places to the State (Tolan 1). This development is a clear proof of the hesitation "between separation of the State from religious affairs and a desire to shape and influence French Islam" (Tolan 49). As Fernando has convincingly argued, the fact that the state was a major player in the creation of the CFCM goes against the principle of secularism (6). Fernando demonstrates that secularism in France is more about "the imbrication of religion and politics rather than their separation, about active state management rather than neutrality, and about the production and regulation of religious subjects rather than simply the guarantee of their freedom." She considers "recent laws against veiling (usually understood as repressive tactics) and the state's establishment of institutions like the French Council on the Muslim Religion and the Institute for the Cultures of Islam (usually understood as inclusionary gestures) as part of an array of disciplinary techniques aimed at cultivating properly religious (that is, secular) Muslim subjects" (Fernando 20).

Another way to look at the issue is that Islam lags behind compared to other long-established religions in France, and its followers do not have the means to catch up in a timely manner. Muslims lack adequate infrastructure to accommodate some of their ritual practices, and this is where a body such as the CFCM can play a role along with the state, since pressing needs require state or local authorities' approval such as permits to build mosques, to sacrifice animals and regulate the meat distribution and sale. Despite the fact that the CFCM continues to be contested, it is an official political recognition of Islam that contributes to inscribing it within the French nation, thus helping to create a French Islam (Zeghal 2), although it has been denounced for recalling the colonial model of dealing with Islam (Zeghal 8).

COMMUNAUTARISME IN SCHOOLS

Contrary to the top-down effort of the French government to organize Islamic institutions in France, the opening of Muslim schools has been a grass-roots movement, and their increasing number has fueled concerns that this is one more sign of Muslims' *communautarisme*. Concerns over *communautarisme* have also surfaced in the context of private Catholic and Jewish schools. For instance, when the 1992 Lang-Cloupet agreement was negotiated, the teachers' union strongly opposed them as concessions made to the Catholic schools that reinforced what they considered to be a communitarian network (Poucet, *Liberté* 182). The debate in the 1990s about secularism did prompt some to wonder about the specific character of some very traditionalist Catholic schools and identity-focused Jewish schools promoting *communautarisme* (Poucet, *Liberté* 184). While Erik Cohen sees the increase in the number and diversity of Jewish schools as a sign of *communautarisme*— though he does not use that term but instead "un repli sur un entre-soi juif" (238)—he insists that this does not stem from a lack of integration. To the contrary, Jews are perfectly integrated in France economically, socially, culturally, and the increased need to delve into Jewish identity takes integration into French society as a given point of departure, not as a goal (278). Nowadays, concerns over *communautarisme* in private confessional schools in the media are always linked to Islam (and sometimes some Christian and Jewish schools, but never Christian and/or Jewish alone).

In addition to the affair of the scarf, some of the debates surrounding Islam in France take place in schools: halal and/or alternative meals in school cafeterias, long skirts, veiled mothers chaperoning field trips. Attitudes have clearly worsened over the past couple of decades: several teachers in a school commented that when they themselves were children, there used to be alternative meals available for them on days when pork was served in the school cafeteria, and it was not an issue at all at the time. This intransigence is one factor that is drawing Muslims out of public schools. Some Muslims explain that their decision to home school their children is not at all a *communautariste* gesture, but a reaction to the public school's lack of recognition of their different religion. One mother explains that she took her decision when her four-year-old daughter came home crying wanting to celebrate Christmas (Puzenat 243).

In a book that assesses the Debré law and that gives voice to key actors at the time, Pierre Tournemire promotes the idea of a new public education system that would be internally diverse over the current dual system of public and private schools, because not having people with different backgrounds know one another from a young age will not build "the conditions needed for future national unity" (Gasol et al. 76–77).[2] Unfortunately, the trend has been going the opposite direction in an exclusionary manner rather than inclusive of diversity in public schools. As John Bowen notes after recalling four cases including the headscarf affair, imams prosecuted for celebrating religious marriages, the marriage annulment in Lille, and the denial of French citizenship for "défaut d'assimilation" or lack of assimilation, "in all these cases, Muslims wished to be treated as was everyone else; it was French politicians who insisted they had to be treated as a separate category of persons" (*Can Islam* 192–193). And in order to do that, they had to pass new laws in some cases.

Double Talk and the UOIF

Tariq Ramadan, who is undoubtedly the most influential Muslim Francophone scholar, has been a controversial figure in France.[3] He has been accused of "double discours" or double-talk, that is saying one thing in front of secular audiences, and another in front of Muslim ones.[4]

Because his grandfather was the founder of the Muslim Brotherhood, Ramadan is always associated with this movement. While some scholars of Islam, such as Olivier Roy, have explained how Ramadan tailors his approach to different audiences, others, such as Gilles Keppel, have accused him of deliberate dissimulation in this double-talk (Bowen 2007: 190). As Bowen analyzes in the notorious episode when Ramadan was confronted by Sarkozy about the issue of stoning women, these accusations of double-talk are baseless, take quotes out of context, and/or fail to show any contradictions (191). If anything during that exchange, Ramadan got into trouble for not engaging in double-talk. As Bowen concludes, "Ramadan's claim that one can be publicly and communally Muslim, and yet also be a good citizen who follows the rules of laïcité *had better be* double-talk or else the entire normative edifice claimed by early twenty-first-century France would look shakier than one might wish" (Bowen 2007: 193).

These accusations of double-talk have been extended to the UOIF and to the schools that are associated with it, because their promotion of a French Muslim citizenship is clearly inspired by Tariq Ramadan, who has been a frequent guest speaker at their annual convention. The Union of Islamic Organisations of France is considered the main out of three major groups of Muslim associations in France; it is constantly under scrutiny for accusations of double talk: that their discourse promoting a French Muslim citizenship hides a will to islamize or bring sharia to French society. As Peter demonstrates, this does not take into account the evolution of the UOIF since its founding in 1983 (108–109; see also Gemie 103–106). The assumption spread by the media and politicians that the UOIF equals Muslim Brotherhood equals fundamentalism "distorts a more complex political and religious reality" (Gemie 104). These accusations spill over onto Muslim schools, because the UOIF has played a role in founding the most visible Muslim schools such as Al-Kindi and Averroès, and maintains strong ties with them. Amar Lasfar, one of the driving forces of Averroès, was president of the UOIF, several high-ranking UOIF members are involved in some Muslim schools, and the first federation of Muslim schools is also tied to the UOIF. But most of the UOIF's members are not motivated by a political project (Gemie 106). When I asked one member of Averroès' administrative team about the strong ties between the school and the UOIF and its political agenda, he laughed and joked that "we have enough troubles managing a mosque, let alone a country." Regardless, the perception is definitely there, as evidenced by the cynical reaction from an employee at the Ministry of Education when I pointed out that several schools present themselves as forming future citizens: "we are told what we want to hear but there is no guarantee that this is what they are doing."

From many Muslims' point of view, they are not asking for specific communal rights, but for what is already their rights under French law, which is the point that scholars who analyzed Ramadan's thought have concluded: "As Ramadan constantly reiterates, he is not asking for special rights for Muslims, but for their liberation through their full participation in French society as Muslims" (Gemie 127). The second part of this book examines whether the founding of Muslim schools can be considered as one example of such full participation.

Notes

1. Some of the criteria included the increasing number of Muslim cultural spaces, wearing oriental and religious clothing, and ethnic businesses.
2. "Si, dès les bancs de l'école, on ne met pas des gens qui ont des sensibilités, des opinions, des origines différentes, on ne crée pas les conditions de l'unité nationale pour demain."
3. For an overview of Ramadan's thinking, see Gemie's chapter.
4. See Bowen (2007) for a discussion of this double talk (189–193).

References

Adida, Claire, David Laitin, and Marie-Anne Valfort. *Why Muslim Integration Fails in Christian-Heritage Societies.* Cambridge: Harvard University Press, 2016.

Arslan, Leyla. "Islam and *Laïcité* in France." *After Integration: Islam und Politik.* Ed. M. Burchardt and I. Michalowski. Wiesbaden: Springer VS, 2015. 187–204.

Beaman, Jean. *Citizen Outsider: Children of North African Immigrants in France.* Oakland, CA: University of California Press, 2017.

Begag, Azouz. *Ethnicity and Equality: France in the Balance.* Trans. Alec Hargreaves. Lincoln and London: University of Nebraska Press, 2007.

Beyer, Caroline. « Troyes: ouverture contestée d'une école musulmane hors contrat. » *Le Figaro*, 15 September 2016.

Bowen, John. *Why the French Don't Like Headscarves: Islam, the State and Public Space.* Princeton, NJ: Princeton University Press, 2007.

Brouard, Sylvain, and Vincent Tiberj. *As French as Everyone Else? A Survey of French Citizens of Maghrebin, African, and Turkish Origin.* Philadelphia: Temple University Press, 2011.

Cesari, Jocelyne. *Why the West Fears Islam: An Exploration of Muslims in Liberal Democracies.* NewYork, NY: Palgrave Macmillan, 2013.
Davidson, Naomi. *Only Muslim: Embodying Islam in Twentieth-Century France.* Ithaca and London: Cornell University Press, 2012.
Dhume-Sonzogni, Fabrice. *Liberté, égalité, communauté : l'État français contre le communautarisme.* Paris: Homnisphères, 2007.
Elmaleh, Raphaël. *Une histoire de l'éducation juive moderne en France. L'école Lucien de Hirsch.* Paris: Biblieurope, 2006.
Fetzer, Joel, and Christopher Soper. *Muslims and the State in Britain, France, and Germany.* Cambridge and New York: Cambridge University Press, 2005.
Fernando, Mayanthi. *The Republic Unsettled: Muslim French and the Contradiction of Secularism.* Durham: Duke University Press, 2014.
Fredette, Jennifer. *Constructing Muslims in France: Discourse, Public Identity, and the Politics of Citizenship.* Temple University Press, 2014.
Gasol, Jean, André Blandin, and Pierre Tournemire. « Des témoins ont la parole II. » *L'Etat et l'enseignement privé: L'application de la loi Debré.* Ed. Bruno Poucet. Rennes: Presses universitaires de Rennes, 2011. 65–83.
Gemie, Sharif. *French Muslims: New Voices in Contemporary France.* Cardiff: University of Wales Press, 2010.
Gresh, Alain. « Pour en finir avec l'adjectif « musulman » (ou « islamique »). » *Le Monde diplomatique,* 3 August 2012. https://blog.mondediplo.net/2012-08-03-Pour-en-finir-avec-l-adjectif-musulman-ou.
Guénif-Souilamas, Nacira. « La Française voilée, la beurette, le garçon arabe et le musulman laïc. Les figures assignées du racisme vertueux. » *La République mise à nu par son immigration.* Ed. Nacira Guénif-Souilamas. Paris: La Fabrique, 2006. 109–132.
Joppke, Christian, and John Torpey. *Legal Integration of Islam: A Transatlantic Comparison.* Cambridge, MA: Harvard University Press, 2013.
Keaton, Trica. *Muslim Girls and the Other France: Race, Identity Politics, and Social Exclusion.* Bloomington: Indiana University Press, 2006.
Laurence, Jonathan. *The Emancipation of Europe's Muslims: The State's Role in Minority Integration.* Princeton: Princeton University Press, 2011.
Laurence, Jonathan, and Justin Vaisse. *Integrating Islam in France: Political and Religious Challenges in Contemporary France.* Washington, DC: Brookings Institution Press, 2006.
Le Guellec, Gurvan. « Les écoles musulmanes sont-elles malvenues? » *Nouvel Obs,* 21 janvier 2017. https://www.nouvelobs.com/education/20170120.OBS4112/les-ecoles-musulmanes-sont-elles-malvenues.html.
Mazawi, André. « "Qui a peur du lycée musulman?" Media Representations of a Muslim School in France. » *Social Semiotics* 19.3 (September 2009): 235–256.
Noiriel, Gérard. *Le creuset français.* Paris: Seuil, 1988.

———. *A quoi sert «l'identité nationale»*. Marseille: Agone, 2007.

Poucet, Bruno. *La liberté sous contrat: une histoire de l'enseignement privé*. Paris: Éd. Fabert, 2009.

Puzenat, Amélie. *Conversions à l'islam*. Rennes: Presses Universitaires de Rennes, 2015.

Roy, Olivier. *Secularism Confronts Islam*. Columbia University Press, 2009.

Seniguer, Haoues. «Communauté, «communautarisme» et islam en France: y a-t-il un «communautarisme» musulman?» *Droit Social* 9 (September 2015): 664–673.

Talpin, Julien, Julien O'Miel, and Frank Frégosi, eds. *L'islam et la cité: Engagements musulmans dans les quartiers populaires*. Villeneuve d'Ascq: PU du Septentrion, 2017.

Thomas, Elaine R. *Immigration, Islam, and the Politics of Belonging in France*. Philadelphia, PA: University of Pennsylvania Press, 2011.

Tissot, Sylvie. «Qui a peur du communautarisme? Réflexions critiques sur une rhétorique réactionnaire.» *lmsi.net*, 23 mars 2016. http://lmsi.net/Qui-a-peur-du-communautarisme.

Tolan, John. «A French paradox? Islam and Laïcité.» *Georgetown Journal of International Affairs* XVIII.2 (Summer–Fall 2017): 41–50.

Zeghal, Malika. «La constitution du Conseil Français du Culte Musulman: reconnaissance politique d'un Islam français?» *Archives de sciences sociales des religions* 129 (January–March 2005). http://assr.revues.org/1113.

CHAPTER 2

Private Education Under Contract

Historical Survey

Old Regime to Post-1789

Before the French Revolution, under the Old Regime, education was under the purview of the Catholic Church. The State did not intervene, and the only schools it supported were those that prepared for military careers (Duval 12). The French Revolution put an end to the Church's monopoly on education, though it would not be fully implemented until the Third Republic due to the political upheavals and alternating of authoritarian and democratic regimes throughout the nineteenth century (Duval 19). The break initiated by the French Revolution is the cause of the political and ideological conflict that marked the nineteenth century, between the France of the Enlightenment and the Catholic Church, both of whom viewed education as a key element to control society (Duval 19). The constitution of 1791 affirmed the principle of public education. In 1833, the Guizot law created a public primary schooling. By declaring that primary schooling must be secular, the third Republic broke with the Church (Duval 22). The French Revolution and the ensuing anti-clerical sentiments marked a break in the field of education, but to this day, the Catholic Church still dominates private education and also influences public education. As Bruno Poucet points out, even the organization and pedagogical principles that govern the French schooling system come from the Catholic Church.[1]

In the early 1800s, there was no distinction between public and private education, and the educational landscape was quite varied. Schools were subject to authorization by the Imperial University, an institution that unlike today's universities, was charged with public education and that delivered authorizations for all teaching institutions (Poucet, "Introduction" 11–12). A few unauthorized schools were quickly shut down and stirred great controversies in 1828 and 1831; these events seem to anticipate the future debate on private education. Various secular laws such as the Guizot and Falloux laws mandating the separation of schools and the Catholic Church in the 1880s did not curb the existing religious schools. There was neither legislation nor oversight on private schools (Poucet, "Introduction" 12).

From 1905 to Post WWII

At the dawn of the twentieth century, private schooling in France was dominated by Catholic schools that were run both by the clergy or lay people (Poucet, "Introduction" 13). The few secular private schools that existed at the time were either niche schools that filled specific vocational needs or that subscribed to specific pedagogies, as well as a few Protestant and Jewish schools (Poucet, *Liberté* 19). The beginning of the 1900s was dominated by what has been called "la guerre scolaire" (the school war) following the 1905 law of separation of Church and State. According to a testimony by Louis Astre, this school war was led by the Church and its conservative allies first to oppose the Third Republic laws about secular education and then, after WWII to get public financing for its network of schools (quoted in Poucet, "La loi Debré" 60). In 1917, the Catholic Church published a decree that forbade Catholic children from attending non-Catholic schools. It later created a special committee (Comité national de l'enseignement libre) in 1931 so that schools could start organizing themselves and join forces (Poucet, "Introduction" 12).

The issue of public funding for private schools was raised as early as the 1920s (Poucet, "Introduction" 15). In 1929, the union for primary school teachers expressed its desire to see the nationalization of all private schools (Poucet, "Introduction" 16). At the eve of WWII, private schools were educating about one quarter of the student population, forty percent of them in secondary schools (Poucet, *L'enseignement* 33). By 1939, the issue of private schooling was one subset of the highly charged wider question of the relationship between the Church and the

State, each party trying to gain back what they lost when the Concordat was terminated in 1905 (Poucet, *Liberté* 27).

During WWII, the Vichy government allocated some funding for elementary private education, but that was stopped at the end of the war (Poucet, *Liberté* 27). Pétain also allowed the Congregations to teach again (which they had been forbidden to do in 1904), as well as catechism (Poucet, *L'enseignement* 33). The immediate post-WWII period was marked by some rapid changes: a higher demand for education and an increased duration of school attendance beyond the compulsory minimum age. Between academic years 1945–1946 and 1957–1958, the percentage of schooled children aged 12–15 years more than doubled from 20.5 to 44%, with a sharp increase in the total numbers of students at the elementary level, in both private and public schools (Langouët 170). Moreover, in 1946, only 23% of the population was in favor of public subsidies for private education, but that number doubled to 46% in just five years (Langouët 170).

1959: The Debré Law

In 1959, mandatory schooling was extended to the age of 16. In post-WWII France, the modernization of the school system could not have happened in some parts of the country, particularly the West where private schools dominated given the sharp increase in the number of children in schools (Langouët 170). There was an awareness that private schools were providing a service to the community at large. In 1959, there were 7 million students, including 1.8 million in private schools, among them 1.6 million spread into 14,000 Catholic schools. France counted 20 Protestant schools and 5 Jewish ones, and 310 non-religious private schools educated 100,000 students (Poucet, *Liberté* 74–75). Non-religious private education was very small, it included schools with specific pedagogical approaches such as Montessori and Steiner. Protestant and Jewish schools were few (15 Jewish schools in 1961). Indeed, in Poucet's account, all references to negotiations with the government mention representatives from the Catholic Church only, and none from other faith-based institutions.

The Debré law is a watershed moment in the history of private schooling in France for several reasons. For the first time, it established a relationship between the State and private schools (Visse 488). As historians and scholars point out in a paradoxical phrasing, this law created "un service privé d'enseignement public" or "private service of public schooling" (Langouët 170). Moreover, as Poucet notes, the law catalyzes several issues at the core of French society's values, and that beyond the political question hides a cultural one, with debates between the singular and the universal, between unity and diversity that resonate particularly strongly in contemporary French society ("La loi Debré: une histoire" 26). The aim of this chapter is simply to explain the history and current debates around private schooling, not to engage in the debate as to whether it is a private service of public utility or not, but insofar as it relates to the recent phenomenon of Muslim schools. But Poucet's question is pointed: is private education under contract a specific modality or a questioning of the meaning and value of public education (Poucet, "Introduction" 18)? Several people in charge of Muslim schools insisted that they are one modality of the national education system.

As Langouët insists repeatedly, one cannot really talk about private education for the schools that are under contract with the State because they function as a "service privé d'enseignement public" (181). Given the extent of public subsidies (from the State and local administrations) to private schools in general, one is justified to wonder what is left as private, as does Toulemonde ("La naissance" 453). Tapernoux points out that teachers in the private sector are a very heterogeneous group, and that they are facing the same issues as their colleagues in the public schools, though the media tends to emphasize the differences rather than the convergences (267–269).

In his book that details the various steps and negotiations that led to the Debré law, Poucet explains that the law was conceived as a compromise meant to end the fight between, on the one hand, the proponents of Catholic schools (who believed were providing a service to the community), and, on the other hand, those for whom the separation of Church and State made it unlawful for the State to subsidize religious schools to the detriment of public schools (*Liberté* 75–89). Signed into law on December 31, 1959, the Debré law ended the "school war", which was a political and cultural war, but neither party was happy about it: this is a law imposed by the State to consolidate the State (Poucet, "La loi Debré" 26–31). In any case, the law forced some public control over Catholic schools. As a result, a few schools refused to go under contract because they felt that the law did not allow for schools to be "Catholic enough" (Poucet, "La loi Debré" 42).

One of the compromises was the recognition of the "caractère propre" "specific character" of private schools, mentioned in Article 1 of the law, but never defined, because any acknowledgment of difference breaks with the universal ideals of the French Revolution that are deemed essential to guarantee equality (Poucet, *Liberté* 91). The specific character of a school can be religious or pedagogical. At the time, there was an unofficial quota mentioned: private schooling should not exceed 20% of all schooled children (Jean Gasol, quoted in Poucet, "La loi Debré" 67).

There is a stark contrast between the Debré law (which was enabled in part by a context of increased demand for school seats due to demographic increase and a concern to preserve national unity), and follow-ups added in the 1970s as a political response from the right to the specific politics of the time (Visse 488–489). The right who was in power passed measures that favored the private sector and not the public one, subject to protests since 1968. The Debré law was temporary and scheduled to be reviewed, but this review was slightly delayed by the events of 1968. Eventually, the Debré law was made definitive or perpetuated in 1971; it was followed by the Guermeur law that established equity between teachers in the public and private sectors and also reaffirmed the specific character of each school in 1977.

Contracts

Under the Debré law, schools must operate for a period of five years before they are eligible for a contract with the State. The law allows a choice between two types of contract: a simple contract (contrat simple), more aligned with the private schools' demands at the time, or a partnership contract (contrat d'association), more aligned with the State's demands. The simple contract, only available nowadays to elementary schools, allows schools to exert more control over their teachers who are paid directly by the State. The curriculum must follow the national curriculum but with some freedom; the State checks teachers' qualifications and conducts evaluations. This simple contract has been chosen by about one quarter of private schools. Under simple contract, the city may cover all or parts of the operations budget (but not exceed the amount allocated to public schools) (Poucet, *L'enseignement* 106–109), though local authorities have no financial obligation toward helping schools under simple contract (Toulemonde 113–114). According to Poucet's book published in 2012, thirty percent of private primary schools under contract are under this simple contract (*L'enseignement* 77). The partnership contract has been the only contract that secondary schools have been eligible for since a change in regulations in 1980 (Poucet, *L'enseignement* 77). In the partnership contract (the most popular), teachers are recruited, paid and evaluated by the State (Toulemonde 114). In the contract, there are two different statuses for teachers: they can be State employees, or contract employees with the state, and these two statuses have been at the heart of a power struggle between the State and (mostly Catholic) private institutions. Local authorities contribute for some operational expenses at the same level as for the public schools. Schools must follow the national curriculum. The shift in teachers' compensation changed the fact that individual schools are no longer the direct employer of its teachers (Poucet, "La loi Debré" 33). Some support staff salaries are also covered by the State (see Poucet, *L'enseignement* 106–109 for additional details). In addition, there are indirect subsidies that are given directly to families by the local administration for transportation, school supplies, field trips, etc.

Not all private schools select to sign a contract with the State, in this case they are described as "hors contrat" "non-contracted school." This label can be misleading as the term is applied to both schools who elect to stay completely independent and schools who are still in the probationary period before they are eligible to apply for a contract. Nonetheless, non-contracted schools are subject to some basic regulations regarding the need to provide a sanitary environment, morality, and competency, but have total pedagogical freedom (Poucet, *L'enseignement* 3). Since 2006, they also have to follow the nationally mandated common core and competency requirements (Poucet, *L'enseignement* 77). Some schools elect to remain without a contract for a variety of reasons, including the fact that according to them, being under contract stifles pedagogical innovation (Poucet, *L'enseignement* 94).

Over the years, there is a constant pull between association or parity of private with public education, but various laws added to the Debré one (such as the Chevènement law in 1985) reinforce the idea that the public comes first (Toulemonde, "La naissance" 451). Modifications made to the Debré law show a constant equilibrium between unity and diversity, equity and association of the private and public sectors, with no way to tell where the balance will tilt in the future (Toulemonde, "La naissance" 451). Since the Debré law, teachers' status has been a constant point of contention between the State and private schools (mostly Catholic). In 1992, the Lang-Cloupet agreements aligned the recruitment of teachers with the recruitment and training in the public sector, notably with the creation of a national *concours* or competitive exam (CAFEP) similar to the CAPES for public schools (Toulemonde, "La naissance" 448–449). Nonetheless, some of the questions surrounding the issue that subsides in terms of teachers' status are as follows: Are teachers either State employees (known as fonctionnaires) or contract public servants (contractuel de droit public)? Are they under the leadership of the institution where they teach or under the State? Must they adhere to the specific character of their school? (Toulemonde 114–123).[2]

Impact

When taking stock of the Debré law, Antoine Prost states that it indisputably stopped the decline of private education, particularly at the secondary level. He reminds us that both private and public secondary schools were in competition as they both charged tuition until 1930 when public secondary schools were made free. The private sector accounted for half of students as attested by various commissions in 1899 and 1940. After WWII, private schools could not compete with the public schools that were now free, especially given the fact that students stayed longer in school; their share right before the Debré law was enacted had fallen to below a quarter of all students (Prost 315). The Debré law had purposefully limited the subsidies to existing schools so as to prevent the creation of new ones (Prost 316). Another point he makes is that subsidies are conditional to the recognition for a proven need: should public schools suffice to school all children, a contract is not justified (Prost 316), hence the requirement for schools to operate on their own for five years before being eligible to apply for a contract.

Second Half of Twentieth–Twenty-First Century

Starting in the 1970s, private schooling no longer fulfils just a need or desire for religious education, but can vary from a wish to avoid mixing with different social classes to give a second chance to students (Poucet, *Liberté* 154). For those unfamiliar with the French system, it should be noted that contrary to the U.S. one, holding students back a year is a common practice, and that particularly at the time, students could be counselled into vocational education as early as the end of seventh grade regardless of the family's wishes. In this very selective and elitist system, private schooling slowly evolved from religious education to being now labelled free choice education (enseignement libre). Hence, any attack on private schooling would be construed as an attack on freedom of school choice (Poucet, *Liberté* 155) something that Minister of Education Alain Savary would find out the hard way.

1984

With the election of president François Mitterrand in 1981, the Minister of Education was tasked with fulfilling Mitterrand's campaign promise to make of "the National Education a great, unified, and secular public service" "un grand service public unifié et laïque de l'Education nationale," though the formula was ambiguous enough to lead itself to different implementations (Visse 489). Although Mitterrand's Socialist party was in control of the National Assembly, the government failed to take advantage of the moment and engaged in lengthy consultations and debates to elaborate the Savary bill. On June 24, 1984, one million people demonstrated in Paris, chanting "private schooling will live on" "l'école libre vivra" to protest Savary's project. Demonstrators included people politically aligned with the left as well as parents of children in public schools (Poucet, *Liberté* 166–167). Despite debate about the exact figures (between 1.6 and 1.8 million), this was at the time the largest demonstration in French history (Poucet, "La loi Debré" 69), and it forced the government to back down and withdraw the bill. As Visse points out, public opinion was clearly for the status quo as more and more people want the option to put their children in private schools, with an emphasis on consumer choice rather than social bonds (491).[3]

Numbers

Since 1959, private schooling has decreased in share: in 1957–1958, 40% of secondary students were in private schools (among whom 34% in Catholic schools) (Gasol et al. 76); this number has dropped by half in about a fifty-year span. According to the Ministry of education, in 2011–2012, about 17% (2,084,400 students) of pupils in France (roughly 13% for elementary schools and 21% in secondary schools), attended

8800 private schools (representing about 13.6% of the total number of schools); 98% of these students attended a school under contract with the state. Tournemire confirms this declining trend, from 42% of secondary students in the 1957–1958 school year, including 34% in Catholic schools, down to 21% in secondary schools in the late 2000s. These numbers are the same for 2015: 2 million students educated in 8800 schools.

The State does not keep track of whether a school is confessional or not, but it is obvious that private schooling in France is still overwhelmingly dominated by the Catholic schools (95%), the remaining 5% is shared by the Jewish, Protestant, Muslim and non-religious schools (Tapernoux 5). Over the years, there has been a progressive secularization of Catholic schools through the personnel (teachers, directors…) who are overwhelmingly secular and not religious or priests (Toulemonde, "naissance" 456). Moreover, a survey conducted in 1993–1994 showed that only 42% of students enrolled in Catholic schools attended catechism: therefore, a Catholic education is no longer the main motivation for the majority of families enrolling their children in Catholic schools (Poucet, *L'Etat* 103). Indeed, a small minority of schools do not pursue a contract because it does not, in their opinion, allow them to be Catholic enough (Poucet, "La loi Debré" 42).

According to statistics published in 2008, 8000 Catholic schools taught 2 million children, 256 Jewish schools 30,000 children, and 5 Muslim schools 600 students (this last one is probably the most outdated number)[4]; 98% of students in private schools attend a school under contract with the State, but only a handful of Islamic schools have succeeded so far in getting funded by the French government. Given that France's Muslim population is estimated between 3 and 6% of the population (Western Europe's largest Muslim population), one can see that Muslim schools are lagging behind, due to several factors, including the fact that Islam is a relative new comer, its population was immigrant until relatively recently, and prevalent discrimination against many new Islamic institutions.

Recent developments include a sharp increase in the number of non-contracted schools, such as the movement « créer son école » (create your school)[5] founded by Anne Coffinier that has opened 450 schools in a five-year span (Toulemonde 124). As Bruno Poucet points out, for-profit schools are thriving and seem to provoke fewer objections than faith-based schools, particularly Muslim schools ("La loi Debré" 42).

Geographical Disparities

National statistics can hide striking disparities in some geographical areas linked to various historical factors. For instance in 1971–1972, the proportion of private education in the academy of Strasbourg was 5.9% versus 43.6% in Rennes (Langouët and Léger 27), which can be explained by the strong presence of the Church and Catholic practice in that region. Britany also stands out by the fact that children of senior executives and managers (cadres supérieurs) are more likely to go to the public sector than in other areas (Langouët and Léger 106).

Another peculiar situation is found in Alsace-Moselle, where religion is taught in both private and public schools. Parents have the option to opt out of it, and public schools can be religious schools if they follow one of the four recognized faiths: Catholic, Lutheran, Calvinist, and Jewish. These departments follow regulations of the Concordat that were in place prior to their annexation by Germany in 1871. The 1905 law of separation of Church and State were not implemented following Alsace-Moselle's reintegration into the French nation after WWI because of strong local opposition (Poucet, *L'enseignement* 97).

Zapping

According to Langouët and Léger, there has been a noticeable increase in the percentage of families resorting to private schools for at least one of their children, with more than 40% of families doing so (11). In 1995–1996, out of 100 students, 59 went only to public schools, 6–7 only to private schools, and almost 35 went to both from the beginning of elementary to the end of secondary schools (Langouët 179). This has led to the observation that "zapping" or switching from public to private and/or vice versa has become more popular, and is indicative of the fact that both sectors have become, in the eyes of families, complementary (Langouët 179).

In their study, Langouët and Léger demonstrate that the majority of families with children in private schools are doing so as a remedy for failure in the public system, and that those who are doing so solely out of religious reasons or other motivations linked to the specific character of the school are a minority. In their longitudinal studies, they show that the rate of use of the private sector is actually higher than what is shown by transversal studies that do not account for transfers between the two, or what they label as zapping (56). In the case of families who go back and forth between private and public, the recourse to private school is most likely a response linked to failure and not an ideological or religious motivation (Langouët and Léger 61–62). Indeed, the majority of cases of transfers from public to private comes in response to a school's decision to have a student repeat a year (Langouët and Léger 118). However, this finding is disputed by François Héran who points out, using additional data, that there is a strong correlation between the religious practice of parents and the choice of a confessional school and concludes that the impact of academic failure is much less than the religious factor (29–31).

Budget

I met with someone in charge of private education in the Direction des affaires financières (DAF) (financial affairs) in the Ministry of Education in Spring 2018, to get a better understanding of the Ministry's stand point regarding private education, and the place of Muslim schools. He explained to me that private schooling was under the umbrella of the budget office because historically the relationship between the government and private schools has been a financial relationship, therefore the DAF has been charged with it. In 2006, in the context of a budgetary redistribution, it was suggested that private schooling be placed under a different umbrella, but neither the DGRH (Human Resources) nor the DGESCO (Direction générale de l'enseignement scolaire) agreed to take it in. So the DAF remained the principal administrative center for private schools but the pedagogical aspect was put under the responsibility of the DGESCO.

Private education (both primary and secondary levels) represents 11% of the total budget of the Ministry of Education. Out of this, 90% goes toward teachers' salaries and 10% to non-teaching staff. The Debré law does not stipulate anything regarding the oft-mentioned yet unwritten rule of the 20% ratio between private and public students. In a handout,[6] he noted that if the 20% ratio has been stable over the years, it does not mean that it is a strict rule nor is it immutable, and that it might evolve in the future according to the weight of each sector. In tables showing data between 2007 and 2018, the ratio has remained pretty steady, from the lowest point at 19.86% in 2013–2014 with steady growth up to the highest at 20.19% in 2017–2018.

The balance that needs to be struck between the public and the private sector also needs to take into account the additional means that are allocated to schools that are designated "Education prioritaire" (priority education) which only concerns public schools. Schools with such a designation have a high concentration of children from underprivileged backgrounds and with significant lacunae and academic failure.

Contracts depend not only on a recommendation from the academy but also upon the budget. In recent history, there were 1000 additional teaching positions for 2017, but none in 2018. Every year, there are many more requests than there are positions available, and he stressed that the decision-making process is based on numbers ("logique arithmétique" arithmetical logic) as much as possible. Each network representative does send a prioritized list to the ministry, who is aware, for instance, of the fact that the FNEM claims many schools despite the fact that they have refused to join the association. So, the Ministry takes into account not only the lists presented by the networks, but also by individual schools. When I asked how the Ministry prioritizes the request for new contracts, I was told that these are the criteria they look at:

- how long classes have been open for
- number of students in the class
- if this concerns a particular segment, such as failing students or handicapped students (Instituts Médico-Educatifs for instance that cater to mentally handicapped children)
- balance among the various networks of schools.

The DAF makes recommendations to the Ministry, then final decisions that do not always follow these recommendations are taken at a higher level. Typically, the state covers a substantial amount (at least 80%) of the cost of operating a school when all its classes are under contract.

The Gatel Law

In February 2018, private education was making headlines with a new bill being introduced in the Senate regarding schools that are not under contract. One article points out that this is a marginal phenomenon, since it concerned only 65,000 students in 2017 out of a total of 12 million (Battaglia). While the law will apply to all schools, the language of the debate that surrounded it often seemed to target Muslim schools. Proponents of the bill often referred to the case of Al-Badr school, closed in 2016 for non-compliance in the curriculum (but reopened since then). As Makhlouf Mamèche points out as president of the FNEM (National federation for private Muslim education), the reference to Al-Badr stigmatizes Muslim schools, and the use of arguments such as "preventing radicalization" confirms that concerns about Muslim schools are behind it, even though they are not the only ones who are causing controversies. During the debate in February 2018 at the Senate, Senator Jean-Claude Carle stated that the main goal of the bill was to target "the risks of radicalization, or more broadly of sectarian drift."[7] In fact, Muslim schools constitute a mere 8% of all schools that are not under contract, and 8 out of 10 new schools opened in 2017 are not religious schools (Battaglia).

This bill was debated at the National Assembly during my second visit in March 2018 and the schools I visited expressed a clear sense that Muslim schools were targeted. One of the Muslim school directors I spoke with found it very pertinent to update old laws but couldn't help being uncomfortable with the fact that this was taking place in the context of a surge of Muslim schools. In addition, he pointed out several troubling points. Currently, the procedure to open a school has very clear deadlines in case someone voices opposition, which is dealt with by the Academy, but with the new bill it would be a tribunal that deals with oppositions, and that could take up to four years to get resolved, thus making it much easier to delay the opening of a school. Moreover, the law is not necessarily updating what should be: for instance, someone who has worked as a school monitor is allowed to open a school, which should no longer be considered sufficient qualification. Fatih Sarikir, the president of a new Muslim federation (UEPM) launched a petition with a video to oppose the bill in which he says very explicitly that this is targeting Muslim schools.[8] Another Muslim school administrator labelled the law a "fungicide for Muslim schools" (Interview 2018). Another school director stressed that the Badr school did not respect the law and does not want his community to position itself as a victim. Interestingly, he strongly believes that public school is ultimately the solution, and wishes parents would invest themselves in the public as they do in the private system (as one example, he cited the 100% participation rate of parents whenever his school has parents–teachers conferences).

My original appointment with the Ministry of Education was moved because the bill was on the agenda for the next day at the National

Assembly. This bill was the number one priority for his department, and as a person closely involved in its drafting, he had only positive points to mention about it: this bill would bring up to date and harmonize three laws that are, for the youngest, 99 years old. It will allow for better means in addition to hygiene and good morals (bonnes moeurs) to prevent people who have been convicted of various offenses such as drug trafficking and fraud among other things, as well as ensure that the Common Core (socle commun) is taught. When I asked what his thought was about the fact that Muslim schools feel unfairly targeted because the example given is the closing of Al-Badr in Toulouse, he answered that this law was not targeting Muslim schools but also schools pedagogically deficient, and gave the example of the Angélus school (affiliated with the fundamentalist Catholic network St Pie X, which had been closed by the local authorities (préfet). In addition to better vetting the opening of new schools, the second contribution of the bill is to add systematic control. This official highlighted to me that when it comes to Muslim schools, the Ministry has not changed its stance, but public opinion has.

School Networks

According to the Ministry of Education, the current arrangement works very well and there is no overarching desire in the government to change the current situation. In addition to the Catholic network and smaller Jewish and secular networks, he highlighted the emerging Muslim network, the Protestant network with more and more Evangelical schools, and the regional languages schools which are extremely small numerically but weigh considerably in local politics. Catholic schools were the ones who fought for the Debré law, but this also benefited other faiths' schools. While almost 97.35% of private schools under contract are Catholic, the next runner up are Jewish schools which represent 1.25%, and secular schools (1.25%), Protestant (0.1%), and Muslim (0.02%) according to 2011 data (Poucet, *L'enseignement* 96).

In terms of schools not under contract, the numbers differ greatly: only about 70 schools for Catholic, but 25 Jewish, 20 Protestant, and 9 Muslim (Poucet, *L'enseignement* 90). While most of the Jewish schools that are not under contract are by choice, it is not the case for the Muslim ones. In order to better understand the development of Muslim schools, I turn to a brief history of two other minority faiths in France, to compare how they fared.

Jewish Schools

History and Evolution

Historically, Jewish schools have been closer to public schools and Protestant schools because of the anti-Judaism stance of the Church throughout the nineteenth and first half of the twentieth centuries (Elmaleh 424). In his history of modern Jewish education in France through the spotlight on Lucien de Hirsch school as emblematic of Jewish schools in France, Raphaël Elmaleh explains that the first modern Jewish school, opened in Bordeaux in 1817, was based on the model of a Protestant school that offered guidance in the same city (45). Paradoxically, from the nineteenth to the first half of the twentieth century, both Protestant and Jewish schools felt closer to the secular public school system than to the Catholic one that did not hide its contempt to the two minority faiths. In the case of Judaism, this was exacerbated by the different views on the Revolution and its consequences, beneficial for Jews who were granted citizenship, but detrimental to the Catholic Church that was stripped of much of its power.

From their founding starting in the 1860s till the 1930s, the schools of the Jewish Consistory were quite successful and served the indigent population. In fact, the trend that dominated was to establish Jewish (mostly primary) schools for the poor, and send the other students in other schools (Elmaleh 44). In the first decades of the twentieth century, the majority of children in Consistory schools came from Russia, Romania, and Alsace-Lorraine, and after WWI Poland, Germany, and Austria as well (Elmaleh 83).

The Consistory also supported the publishing of textbooks and religious materials for use in the schools (Elmaleh 64). Jewish education consisted of Biblical Hebrew, ancient Jewish history, and moral lessons derived from the Tora (Elmaleh 89). The school observed Jewish holidays as well as early release on Fridays to allow for Shabbat observance (Elmaleh 112). One telling detail: in the 1920s–1930s, boys are shown on pictures wearing a béret: this is symbolic of the harmony of the Franco-Judaism promoted during that period: the head is covered per Jewish precepts, but with a quintessentially French head cover (Elmaleh 109). This detail is telling of the Hirsch school philosophy of reconciling religious tradition with modern culture that dominated before the war over what will later become an identity affirmation (258). New fashion trends have displaced the béret. Nowadays, the baseball cap has become the traditional substitute for the kippa (Elmaleh 470), as could already be seen on some pictures in Erik Cohen's study where young boys wear a mix of kippas and hats (28).

In the 1930s, one can already see a turn that will be definitive after WWII: Jewish schools move from catering to the poor to focusing on fostering Jewish identity and safety in the context of a failing public school system. In 1935, the creation of the junior high school Maïmonide marks a turning point, as it was the first Jewish secondary school that aimed to provide a high-level general and Jewish education (Elmaleh 163). While social integration had dominated till then, a new preoccupation of rejudaization started to take over (Elmaleh 164).

WWII marked a turning point in Jewish life in France. Waves of refugees from Central Europe, but also later on Egypt and North Africa, changed the French Jewish landscape by bringing religion and observing religious practices back to the forefront (Elmaleh 224). In 1962, Algerian immigration tipped the scale and made the French Jewish population more Sephardi than Ashkenazi (Elmaleh 377). Moreover, the creation of the state of Israel had an impact on Jewish schools and their curriculum: as both Israel and the USA played a fundamental role in the reconstruction of French Judaism post-WWII, Israel took center stage in the curriculum and life of Jewish schools. Starting in the 1970s, Jewish education became a strategic stake not only for identity and demographic reasons, but also for political ones, especially for Israel (Elmaleh 400). The centrality of the state of Israel for French Jews is emphasized by Erik Cohen, who notes that various surveys and studies have shown that for 95% of Jews, Auschwitz and the state of Israel summed up their Jewish identity. Another survey among the leadership of the Jewish community revealed that attachment to Israel was the pillar of Jewish identity in France and that cultivating it was the main objective of a Jewish education (Erik Cohen 44–45, 59).

In 1957–1958, there were few Jewish schools. There was a sharp increase: from 400 students in a dozen schools after WWII to 30,000 students in 2002, thanks to the opening of 35 schools between 1962 and 1980, and 53 school networks founded after 1980 (Elmaleh 555–556). At the turn of the twenty-first century, 25% of Jewish school-aged children attended a full-time Jewish school (Elmaleh 556). Martine Cohen situates the exponential increase in full-time Jewish schools with the notable movement in France starting in the 1970s of Jewish identity affirmation (237). According to her rough estimates, the 30,000 students in Jewish schools represent about one-third of Jewish school-age children, while another third is in Catholic schools and the other third in the public system (237). In 2001, Lucien de Hirsch had 1159 students enrolled, from preK-12, with 2000 students on a waiting list, testimony to its success.

Scholars have pointed out that the notion of community and/or "repli communautaire" (withdrawal into one's community) can be seen among some of the Jewish population. While Catholic schools have become more and more secular during the last decades, thus following an overall secular trend in society at large, an inverse movement can be observed in Jewish schools: an increased focus and priority given to religion (Elmaleh 543). Martine Cohen underlines that the evolution of Jewish schools is tied to the changing context of Jews in French society following their emancipation in 1791, shifting from targeting integration to a post-integration identity affirmation ("dynamique identitaire 'post-intégration'" (238). This is echoed by Elmaleh, who points out that in 1900, foreign parents wanted their Jewish children to become French and assimilate, whereas a century later, parents who are French by birth and by education want their children to become Jewish, though, in most cases, the identity motivation takes second place to the desire for a high-quality education in a safe environment that public schools are deemed inadequate to offer (408). Elmaleh notes a phenomenon of dual communitarian and social withdrawal ("phénomène de renfermement (repli à la fois communautaire et social)" in the 1970s–1980s, with enrollments doubling in 15 years to reach about 25 thousand students in 2000 (407). However, in terms of percentage, the number of children schooled in Jewish schools relative to the Jewish population in France remains roughly the same between the turn of the twentieth and the twenty-first century (Elmaleh 408).

Diversity

Jewish schools are concentrated in Paris and its suburbs; and 64% of schools and 71% of their students are Sephardi (E. Cohen 52). Jewish schools are extremely diversified, spanning a spectrum ranging from the strictest ultra-Orthodoxy to a more cultural Judaism, and including a modern orthodoxy that takes several forms. According to Martine Cohen, these three key focus differentiate themselves by two main features of school life: the type of Jewish education that is offered in terms of content and its importance compared with general education, and the level of religious practice demanded in the school regarding co-ed and dress code and potentially in the family (245).

In what Martine Cohen labels as "ultra-orthodox pole," which she defines as a strict observance of religious commands, there is separation of the sexes from KG, dress code for girls mandates long dresses or skirts with arms and legs fully covered, kippa for boys, and covered hair for married female teachers (M. Cohen 246). In the Haredi network, religious observance is also expected from parents. Jewish education can take up to 15 hours a week, time is allocated daily for prayers, and the school calendar observes religious holidays (M. Cohen 246). At the other end of the spectrum is the "cultural pole", with modern Hebrew and a minimum of religious rules such as Kosher food in the cafeteria, and where Jewish education does not exceed 4–6 hours a week and is mostly about Jewish history and only includes biblical references when they serve as founding myths for the state of Israel (M. Cohen 247). Erik Cohen found that the most important group of Jewish schools in France (30 schools enrolling 47% of students), which he labels traditionalist-Zionist, celebrate the day that marks the Independence of Israel and require wearing the kippa (78).

In his study, Erik Cohen found that gender separation was applied in half of preschools and most elementary schools, in about 80% of middle and 65% of high schools (76). Also 86% of Jewish schools required wearing the kippa at school (76). Some schools, such as those belonging to the Ozar Hatorah network, mostly admit halakhic (that is practicing) children (E. Cohen 73–74).

E. Cohen notes that the repartition of Jewish schools is aligned with private schools in general, with the secondary level being twice the size of elementary which is itself twice and a half the size of preschool. He notes a new trend in the last decade (the 1980s given the date of publication of his study): the development of elementary education is higher than the development of secondary education (141). The Loubavitch movement actually prioritizes preschools because of its belief that the formation of a Jewish identity should start at the youngest age (Elmaleh 559). We see a similar development with some Muslim schools.

Parents' Motivations

Elmaleh's assessment is that "Jewish school used to transform little Jews into little French people, nowadays it is tasked with changing little French into little Jews."[9] When M. Cohen told school directors about this statement, several disagreed with the second half of the statement, stressing that they educate children as much about citizenship as about Judaism, while others argued about the need to preserve Jewish identity from an assimilating society or the difficulties to reach out to a Jewish population ignorant of its heritage (M. Cohen 249).

According to interviews with various school directors, the main motivation for parents to send their children to a Jewish school is linked to a Jewish identity formation "motivation identitaire juive" (M. Cohen 251), a protected Jewish environment that facilitates religious observance such as the Shabbat and religious holidays, friendships with other Jewish children and in the long term mitigate the risk of a mixed marriage. Others focus on the transmission of a Jewish identity that can range from respecting more or less religious rules to a sense of belonging, with Israel and modern Hebrew as frames of reference. The majority of parents' motivations is made up of a variable mix of all these reasons (M. Cohen 251). Since 1990, one additional reason is to avoid the public school system and its perceived degradation, and since 2000, fear for safety due to the rise of anti-Semitic acts (M. Cohen 251). Again another parallelism that can be made with Muslim parents sending their children to Muslim schools.

Jewish schools are also confronted to some recent developments that affect society at large, such as blended families, single parents, failing students, and economic challenges. These add to the search for an identity togetherness ("entre-soi identitaire") a search for a social togetherness ("entre-soi social"), thereby problematizing any identity affirmation as a communitarian withdrawal ("repli communautaire") (M. Cohen 254). That is, parents try to find a school that not only provides reinforcement of Jewish identity, but that also caters to families of a similar socioeconomic status. In general, only 18% of families chose private schooling for religious reasons (the majority chose it for discipline and results/performance), but the majority of Jewish families who choose Jewish schools do so for religious and/or Jewish cultural reasons (E. Cohen 146).

Contracts

Seventy-five percent of students in Jewish schools are in a class under contract (M. Cohen 242), the number of contracts allocated to Jewish schools has risen exponentially: 700 positions between 1960 and 1990, and roughly the same number between 1990 and 2005 (M. Cohen 242). Jewish schools are heavily concentrated in the Parisian area: 58% of schools or 71% of students (M. Cohen 243); 36% of students in Jewish schools are in the academies of Paris, 18% in Créteil, 16% in Versailles, and 11% in Marseille (M. Cohen 243). According to Erik Cohen's figures, it is clear that the geographical concentration of Jewish schools in Paris and surrounding areas follows the distribution of the Jewish population, only 41% of them living in the rest of France (49). Only 42% of Jewish schools are under contract, and 10% have part of their classes under contract (E. Cohen 141); it is safe to surmise that this 10% will eventually be fully under contract, but we are still far from the numbers for Catholic schools.

Until the end of the twentieth century, Jewish schools were almost always in the red (Elmaleh 238), and there would be fewer Jewish schools today if it weren't for the Debré law, a point Elmaleh makes several times in his study (295, 401). In the early days of the Debré law, one could see a different attitude between school directors who were not so enthusiastic about the contract because of the duty to fulfill certain requirements, and between those in charge of school finances who were more amenable to a loss of freedom in exchange of financial help (302). When Lucien de Hirsch school signed a simple contract with the State in 1963, it triggered a significant improvement not only on the material well-being but also on teachers' morale (Elmaleh 306). One should also stress the financial help provided by local governments, particularly by granting the use of municipality-owned land for school construction through 99-year emphyteutic lease ("bail emphytéotique"), as was the case for the Yabné school in Paris' 13th arrondissement in the 1980s among other instances (Elmaleh 402).

Starting in 1967, for the next thirty years, there was a boom in the number of Jewish schools (with emphasis on primary level that was spurred by several factors: financial help through the Debré law contracts, as well as Jewish institutions' proactive help because of the realization that Jewish schooling was essential for the future of Jews in France and for their relationship with Israel (Elmaleh 404). Erik Cohen adds the following factors: the arrival of Sephardic Jews following the decolonization of North Africa, the Six Day War that spurred consciousness of Judaic identity, seeing Jewish schools as a preparation for aliyah, and the perceived degradation of the public sector following 1968 (175–176). The FSJU (Front social juif unifié), created after WWII to rebuild the French Jewish community decimated by the Holocaust, functions as roughly equivalent to the Secrétariat général de l'enseignement catholique, that is as an interface between schools and the government, particularly to negotiate classes under contract. Thus, for instance, the creation of the FIPE (Fond d'investissement pour l'éducation), thanks to an agreement between the Fonds social juif unifié and the Agence juive is a testimony to the priority given to Jewish education. Israel and the US have funded the development of Jewish education in France, through, for instance, the Pincus foundation with donations of more than 20 million francs (E. Cohen 177). Elmaleh notes that it is paradoxical that a part of the Jewish population turned inward in the 1970s–1980s at a time when it was at the height of its integration into French society (Elmaleh 569). In 1990, a special commission was put in place (commission de concertation des écoles juives) to act as a coordinating and representative unit and function as interface with the government (M. Cohen 244–245). This commission represents the Jewish network and organizes the repartition of State contracts among Jewish schools (Poucet, *L'enseignement* 88).

Curriculum

In Catholic schools, religious education takes about 1 hour and a half per week, versus 6–13 hours a week for Jewish education (E. Cohen 141). In the 1950s–1960s, the Lucien de Hirsch's curriculum included 8 hours of weekly religious instruction that included prayers, Biblical and modern Hebrew, and religious holiday celebrations. This religious curriculum was based on the one designed by the Rabbinic school in 1934 (Elmaleh 344–346). According to their website, primary school religious education at Lucien de Hirsch in 2001 consisted of 8 h a week of Kodech plus one optional hour of Yechiva Ketana. Hebrew was taught for an hour and a half a week (Elmaleh 601).

Erik Cohen already noted that teachers for Jewish subjects were a very heterogeneous group in terms of their background and training (from rabbis to former students of a Yeshivot in France, Morocco, or Israel), but in general, their education level is weak, with 50% of them having a high school degree at most (161). Training religious education teachers and developing the content of the religious curriculum are two recurring issues in Jewish schools (Elmaleh 347). In 1992, the André Néher Institute was founded to address the training of teachers. For the teaching of Hebrew, the Agence juive curriculum was adopted (Elmaleh 350). Yet, in 2000, 50% of teachers in charge of Jewish subjects did not have a bachelor's degree and had very little pedagogical experience (Elmaleh 407). According to Elmaleh, training of religious studies teachers and curriculum development for Jewish studies remain the number one priority for Jewish schools (576).

Breach of the Law

The fact that some Jewish schools under contract do not respect some of their obligations under the Debré law has been well documented. These include curriculum and discrimination in admissions. Poucet points out that the State does not react against this (*L'enseignement* 89). For instance, some schools skip Darwin's theory of evolution (Elmaleh 432). Most schools require the religious marriage contract to check that the mother of the child to be registered is Jewish, a clear breach of the Debré law which requires schools to accept all children (Elmaleh 468). In fact, Marianne Picard, the long-time director of Lucien de Hirsch School, wrote a piece in which she opposed accepting children from mixed marriages (Elmaleh 475). Elmaleh notes the tension between the parents for whom academic achievement is the priority and the director who emphasizes Jewish and Zionist education (481). According to Elmaleh, the strong Zionist support advocated by Lucien de Hirsch school is peculiar to that school, and not found in the Loubavitch and Ozar Hatorah schools (515).[10] Martine Cohen confirms that infractions taking place in schools under contract are ignored, and Bernard Toulemonde goes so far as saying that the Ministry had forbidden inspections in Jewish schools (confirmed by Jean Gasol, both cited in the Q&A following Martine Cohen's contribution 260). Gasol emphasizes that there is a lack of political will to address the situation.

In the appendix of his book on Lucien de Hirsch School, Elmaleh copied how the school was presenting itself on its website. Here is one blatant infringement: the morning prayers or Tefila are compulsory for all classes. Moreover, there are gender-specific requirements:

- Starting in 5th grade, Jewish teachings are given separately for boys and girls.
- Girls must wear a dress or a skirt starting in 6th grade.
- Jewish teachings are different at the high school levels in the sense that different emphases are given to boys and girls (emphasis on Michna for girls and on Guemara for boys) (599–602).

These do not make headlines, but it is not an exaggeration to speculate that they would if this was happening in a Muslim school under contract, given recent controversies about Muslim girls' attire (headscarf, long skirts) deemed incompatible with secularism in public schools. Pierre Tournemire's reaction is quite telling when he talks about Jewish schools breaking the Debré law: "People even say that some inspectors do not dare to visit these schools for fear of being accused of antisemitism. And tomorrow Muslim schools which are ramping up!" "On dit même que des inspecteurs n'osent pas, de peur d'être taxés d'antisémitisme, visiter ces écoles. Et demain les écoles musulmanes qui sont en train de monter en puissance!" (cited in Gasol 76). While Tournemire denounces the situation with some Jewish schools, it is immediately tempered by the next statement that portends that Muslim schools will be worse.

Protestant Schools

Protestants have always been a small percentage of the French population, never exceeding 2% (Cabanel and Encrevé 13). Protestants were authorized to open their own schools in 1787 (Poucet 2012). Until the 1880s, public education was denominational; public Protestant schools had their own protestant teachers, students, and catechism complementing the public Catholic schools with their own Catholic teachers, students, and catechism (Cabanel and Encrevé 12). Following the Ferry laws and their secularization of schools, Protestant schools integrated into the public system (Poucet 2012: 3). As Cabanel and Encrevé emphasize, Protestants rallied behind laïcité or secularism not because their religion was closer to its principles, but because as a minority, they always felt threatened by Catholicism and secularism seemed to offer the greatest protection for freedom of religion (18). In 1948, the Fédération protestante de l'enseignement was created as an international and national organization (Poucet 2012: 90). Protestants did not support the Debré law, which they saw as a support for Catholic schools, which they considered incompatible with modernity and democracy (Encrevé 168–169).

In 2010, there were four Protestant (Calvino-Lutheran) schools under contract, and about 20 Evangelical schools not under contract founded in the past few years (Poucet, "Naissance" 264).

Private School and Social Inequalities

While private schools under contract are under obligation to accept all students, in reality, their social make-up is skewed. Toulemonde points out that children of privileged background are overrepresented in the private sector, while those of underprivileged background are underrepresented. Taking as criteria government scholarships (élèves boursiers)[11] solely based on family income, only 16% of students were recipient in the private versus 32% in secondary public schools in 1993–1994. There is a clear social divide between public and private schools: 29% of students in private schools under contract are considered highly privileged and 26.7% are underprivileged, while 18.7% of students in public schools are highly privileged and 40.5% underprivileged (Robert 208).

Whereas religious influence explains the high rate of students schooled in the private sector in Brittany (the two highest rates for the country for the two academies that cover that geographical area), the level of affluence (concentrated in cities) is another determining factor for the location of private schools. Thus, Paris with its 34% rate of students in private schools makes it the third highest in France, whereas the neighboring academy of Créteil, which has a high proportion of low-income families, has among the lowest with 13% (Merle 73). According to Merle, while originally private schools were linked to the influence of the Catholic Church, it has become for those who are socioeconomically privileged (74). Notably, the rate of handicapped children and children classified as experiencing great achievement difficulties (with much need for remediation) is lower in private than in public schools (Merle 75). Looking at data from 2006 to 2010, Merle notices that there is an increase in the proportion of children of disadvantaged background in the public sector while there is a similar increase in the proportion of children of privileged background in the private sector (77).

Private education contributes to social segregation. Private schools are overrepresented when the media publishes the names of the schools with the highest rate of success at the Baccalauréat (high school exam), even though several studies have shown that their students do not progress more than those in public schools if one adjusts to make sure that student characteristics are identical (Merle 71–72). However, Langouët and Léger point out the paradox that characterizes their findings: private schooling is both antidemocratic by its social recruitment but at the same time where students of lower socioeconomic background (at least for the small fraction that does attend private schools) succeed the best. Inversely, the public system is more democratic in its social recruitment initially, but not in the success of children from lower classes, who are more likely to be oriented early and massively toward vocational schools (142). Between the two groups they studied (that is students who entered 6th grade in 1973 and 1974, and then in 1980), Langouët and Léger observed the following changes continued: democratization of the private sector (i.e., more social diversity), and the private sector continued to reduce the gap of success between different social classes at a faster rate (142). Their study showed that the private sector has been more effective in reducing the gap in the rate of success linked to social inequities and in lessening the gap between children of workers and children of executives (134–136). Children of white-collar workers ("employés") are the category that benefits the most from doing a cursus entirely in the private system (Langouët and Léger 123).

This gap is even more pronounced for children of foreign origin who are overwhelmingly schooled in the public system: in elementary schools, more than 97% of them went to the public system and 2% in the private, and in the secondary schools, 93% went to the public and 6% to the private in 1994–1995 (Toulemonde, "La naissance" 456). In his study, Pierre Merle demonstrates how some policies of the Ministry of National education designed to help ZEP (Zones d'éducation prioritaire) schools have actually backfired: while more resources are allocated for schools in ZEP, the distribution of these resources is not even. Thus, some cities of the notorious Seine-Saint-Denis department (including Clichy-sous-Bois), where over 85% of people over 15 do not have a degree, have a rate of schooling children starting at the age of two under the national average (Merle 58). Moreover, the additional cost of priority education, estimated between 10 and 15%, does not take into account the fact that initial spending (consisting mostly of teachers' salaries) is lower in ZEP, which employs younger, less experienced teachers. Thus, the overall budget for ZEP is lower than for downtown schools (Merle 58–59). Academic performance in middle schools designated as "ambition réussite" or RAR (a new category of ZEP schools) has decreased from 2006 to 2009 compared to non-RAR schools (Merle 62–63). RAR middle schools are the most helped of priority education schools, 75% of their students come from lower class and 35% repeat 6th grade (this is twice the national rate) (Merle 64).

In addition to higher teacher turn over, these schools have been suffering increasingly from social and academic segregation: students from middle and upper class background are leaving at higher rates, as well as performing students to the point when in 2009, 33% of the least performing students were schooled in ZEP, compared to 25% in 2003 (Merle 63). Moreover, Merle argues that the very designation of ZEP further stigmatizes those schools by confirming what people on the ground know but is not established for a fact, but the label prompts teachers and middle-class families to leave (64). A similar phenomenon happens with violence in schools, with schools under a plan to curb violent acts that are being tracked since 2002 showing an increase in violence of 29% compared to 9% for other schools (Merle 65). Merle argues that these various labels act in part as a self-fulfilling prophecy and advocates for getting rid of them and concentrating on providing substantial help instead, on the ground that good schools do not need labels to prove their excellence (Merle 67).

Most studies do not point out the intersection of low income and religion in underprivileged areas. Many Muslim schools are located in low-income, socioeconomically depressed neighborhoods. There has not been sufficient attention to the different cultural backgrounds of students for whom a low socioeconomic background is also coupled with a different cultural heritage (with the exception of Dupaire and Mabilon's book), an issue I explore further in Chapter 6.

Conclusion

Private education is still overwhelmingly dominated by the Catholic network, followed far behind by Jewish schools (the second organized network according to Martine Cohen 244), and numerous for-profit and/or particular pedagogy enterprises. It is in this diverse landscape that Muslim schools have emerged in the past two decades. As Poucet has noted, these existing networks and new non-faith-based endeavors do not stir up big controversies. The debate stirred by Muslim schools is part of the larger sociopolitical issue about immigration, Islam in France, and the larger question of national identity that gets fired up during most elections (Poucet, "La loi Debré" 42). Though Jewish networks rarely make headlines, one can see similar patterns and concerns between the development of Jewish and Muslim schools in France: the teaching of a foreign language tied to the religion, and the role (real or imagined) played by foreign countries, allegiances, and agencies.

Notes

1. Such as the authority of the clerics who dispense knowledge (*La liberté* 25).
2. For details about different categories of teachers, see Toulemonde "La naissance," 453–454.
3. "L'heure est au consumérisme scolaire et non à la grande fraternité sur les mêmes bancs."
4. *Revue Enseignement catholique 310, Fonds social juif unifié, Revue Le Monde de l'éducation*, January 2008.
5. See their website http://creer-son-ecole.com/.
6. I had sent a list of my questions prior to our meeting.
7. https://www.senat.fr/seances/s201802/s20180221/s20180221008.html#int948.
8. http://www.ueepm.fr/communique-video-du-president-sur-la-loi-gatel/.
9. "L'école juive transformait hier des petits juifs en petits Français; on lui demande aujourd'hui de métamorphoser de petits Français en petits juifs" (cited in M. Cohen 249).
10. Between 15 and 20% of Lucien de Hirsch's students will eventually move to Israel (Elmaleh 504).
11. Low-income families receive various kinds of financial aid, including subsidized school lunches, "allocation de rentrée scolaire" ("back-to-school scholarship") to help pay for school supplies at the beginning of the school year.

References

Battaglia, Mattea. «L'école privée hors contrat s'invite de nouveau dans le débat politique.» *Le Monde*, 21 February 2018. http://www.lemonde.fr/education/article/2018/02/21/l-ecole-privee-hors-contrat-s-invite-de-nouveau-dans-le-debatpolitique_5260238_1473685.html#qZAwkLL1ZpcThcYT.99.

Cabanel, Patrick, and André Encrevé. «De Luther à la loi Debré: protestantisme, école et laïcité.» *Histoire de l'éducation* 110 (May 2006): 5–21.

Cohen, Erik. *L'étude et l'éducation juive en France. Ou L'avenir d'une communauté*. Paris: Le Cerf, 1991.

Cohen, Martine. « De l'école juive...aux écoles juives. Première approche sociologique. » *L'Etat et l'enseignement privé: L'application de la loi Debré*. Ed. Bruno Poucet. Rennes: Presses universitaires de Rennes, 2011. 237–262.

Durpaire, François, and Béatrice Mabilon-Bonfils. *Fatima moins bien notée que Marianne: L'islam et l'école de la République*. La Tour d'Aigues: L'Aube, 2016.

Duval, Nathalie. *Enseignement et education en France du XVIIIe siècle à nos jours*. Paris: Armand Colin, 2011.

Elmaleh, Raphaël. *Une histoire de l'éducation juive moderne en France. L'école Lucien de Hirsch*. Paris: Biblieurope, 2006.

Encrevé, André. « Les protestants: face à la « loi Debré » de 1959. » *Histoire de l'éducation* 110 (mai 2006): 167–202.

Gasol, Jean, André Blandin, and Pierre Tournemire. « Des témoins ont la parole II. » *L'Etat et l'enseignement privé: L'application de la loi Debré*. Ed. Bruno Poucet. Rennes: Presses universitaires de Rennes, 2011. 65–83.

Héran, François. « École publique, école privée : qui peut choisir? » *Économie et Statistique* 293.1 (1996): 17–39.

Langouët, Gabriel. « L'enseignement privé sous contrat: Continuité, diversité et stabilité. » *L'Etat et l'enseignement privé: L'application de la loi Debré*. Ed. Bruno Poucet. Rennes: Presses universitaires de Rennes, 2011. 169–182.

Langouët, Gabriel, and Alain Léger. *Ecole publique ou école privée? Trajectoires et réussites scolaires*. Paris: Fabert, 1994.

Merle, Pierre. *La ségrégation scolaire*. Paris: La Découverte, 2012.

Poucet, Bruno. *La liberté sous contrat: une histoire de l'enseignement privé*. Paris: Ed. Fabert, 2009.

———. « Introduction: Etat et enseignement privé. » *L'Etat et l'enseignement privé: L'application de la loi Debré*. Ed. Bruno Poucet. Rennes: Presses universitaires de Rennes, 2011. 11–21.

———. « La loi Debré: une histoire en question. » *L'Etat et l'enseignement privé: L'application de la loi Debré*. Ed. Bruno Poucet. Rennes: Presses universitaires de Rennes, 2011. 25–44.

———. *L'enseignement privé en France*. Paris: PUF, 2012.

Prost, Antoine. « Quel bilan tirer de la loi Debré? » *L'Etat et l'enseignement privé: L'application de la loi Debré*. Ed. Bruno Poucet. Rennes: Presses universitaires de Rennes, 2011. 315–320.

Robert, André. « Ecole privée et économie: le poids économique des établissements et la question financière. » *L'Etat et l'enseignement privé: L'application de la loi Debré*. Ed. Bruno Poucet. Rennes: Presses universitaires de Rennes, 2011. 199–214.

Tapernoux, Patrick. *Les enseignants du « privé ». Tribu catholique?* Paris: Anthropos, 2001.

Toulemonde, Bernard. La naissance de «l'» enseignement privé.» *Revue française d'administration publique* 79 (juillet–septembre 1996): 445–459.

———. «La question du contrôle et de la gestion des enseignants du privé.» *L'Etat et l'enseignement privé: L'application de la loi Debré*. Ed. Bruno Poucet. Paris: Rennes: Presses universitaires de Rennes, 2011. 113–130.

Visse, Jean-Paul. *La question scolaire 1975–1984: Evolution et permanence*. Paris: Presses Universitaires du Septentrion, 1995.

PART II

Introduction: Muslim Schools

The introduction to the second part of the book gives numbers and statistics about the growth of Muslim schools in France, and a summary of reactions to that growth. It then explains how field work was conducted in Fall 2016 and Spring 2018, during which I examined materials used in classrooms, observed Arabic and Islamic education classes, and spoke with school administrators and teachers. For the most part, the schools were selected because they were pioneers. The chapters that focus on the schools give an overview of the history, stated goals, and mission of each school on their website, and examine how the schools' objectives translate into practice.

* * *

The first Muslim school established in France is the elementary school Médersa Taalim oul-Islam, founded in the French overseas department of La Réunion in 1947. One must note that it answered a specific need in a context remote from metropolitan France, and as such seems like an exception in the subsequent development that is the focus of this book. Médersa Taalim oul-Islam signed a simple contract with the State in 1970, and a regular contract in 1990. There are no Muslim schools in Mayotte, a recently added overseas department with an important Muslim population, because children go to Qur'anic school in the morning (Poucet, *L'enseignement* 91). I do not take this school into account at all in this book, since it is not part of the recent movement that has been taking place in Metropolitan France, which is the subject of this study.

Full-time Muslim schools opening in Metropolitan France is a very recent phenomenon, which Poucet ties to the law on the headscarf based on chronology and testimonies (Poucet, "Naissance" 266–7). Poucet dates it back to 2001 with La Réussite (and also La Plume, "Naissance" 274), but as we will see in the detailed histories of some schools, the will to do so can be traced back a decade earlier. Poucet correctly notes that the geographical locations of Muslim schools in France maps with immigration from Muslim countries, with strong concentrations in Paris/Ile de France, Lyon, and Lille (*L'enseignement* 102). Poucet's list of Muslim schools opened as of September 2010 totals 11 schools, including two under contract (Médersa and Averroes), catering to 1100 students, among whom only 270 are in classes under contract ("Naissance" 275). All of them are labeled as UOIF, with the exception of the one in La Réunion, La Réussite (linked to Saudi Arabia), La Plume, and Collège éduc'Active (labeled as belonging to the Gülen network). Some of these labels would be disputed by the schools.

Getting public data on religious schools is not an easy task, given that a school does not have to declare a religious belonging. In September 2010, Poucet counted 10 Muslim schools open in metropolitan France ("Naissance" 275), one website counted 31 in 2014, 66 in 2016,[1] another one 86 in 2017.[2] According to figures compiled by the Ministry of Education, in Fall 2017, there were 1192 students in 10 Muslim schools in classes under contract (this was a 17% increase compared to Fall 2016, which was itself an 18% increase compared to 2015). Of these 1192 students, 325 were in the primary level and 867 in the secondary level, and altogether, they represent 0.06% of the roughly 2 million students in classes under contract. In addition, still in 2017, 6586 students were in 64 Muslim schools in classes not under contract, which represent roughly 11% of the total number of students not under contract (Interview March 2018).

This surge is widely seen as a threat. In a radio show on France Info, Representative Éric Ciotti declared that he was preoccupied by this increase.[3] As is often the case, he specified that these schools do not have a contract with the State as if this was a choice on their part, a misleading statement because it is not common knowledge in France that a private school must have operated for five years before being eligible for the contract. Post-interview, Antoine Krempf adds the following details: that the 73,000 students who went to the 1300 schools not under contract in 2017 represent a total increase of 14,000 students and 500 schools in the past seven years, which he admits is an impressive increase, but still a drop given that they represent less than 1% of students. In addition, the increase in the number of Muslim schools is happening at the same rate as non-confessional schools and Evangelical schools. But the latter are not the ones who are raising the bell and the specters of *communautarisme* and radicalization.

In his analysis of the Muslim schools that he listed in 2010, Poucet distinguished two types: first, those that sprang from mosques and that are influenced by either the UOIF (the majority) or the Fédération nationale des musulmans de France (minority), second, those associated with a religious brotherhood. The only example he gives of such schools is Educ'Active (founded in 2009 at Villeneuve-Saint-Georges under the Turkish Gülen movement), but as he rightly notes, there is no Muslim reference on their site (Poucet, "Naissance" 269). Indeed, the school insists that it is a secular school, and there are no markers that they cater to Muslims more than others (no religion nor Arabic language classes). In fact, it insists that the school follows the 2004 law[4] even though as a private school the law does not apply to it. A uniform is compulsory but the website does not give details about it. Poucet's assessment does not see the opening of these schools as a movement "de fond", and that the few schools opening are hesitant between religion and integration[5] (Poucet, "Naissance" 274). I believe that the schools visited for this study do not fit into his schema and sketch a different picture.

The following chapters draw mostly on field work conducted in Fall 2016 and Spring 2018, during which I examined curricula and materials used in classrooms, observed Arabic and Islamic education classes, and talked with school administrators and teachers at several schools. For the most part, the schools were selected because they were pioneers: the first elementary school, the first middle school, the first school to get a contract with the state, etc. This is detailed in each section. I give an overview of the history and of the stated goals and mission of each school, many of which make it a top priority to help students reconcile their identity as Muslim French. I examine how the schools' objectives translate into practice, focusing on how school administrators and teachers endeavor to achieve those goals, particularly through the religion and Arabic classes. I analyze religious education, both similar and different from traditional religious instruction offered in majority-Muslim countries, and see whether these classes do participate in the making of a French Islam.[6]

All of my school visits except one started with a meeting with the director, before I was cleared to go into classes. Some schools responded promptly to my requests, for others I had to be very persistent and kept calling and emailing. This is not meant as a negative comment, but to highlight that they are very busy and do not necessarily have time to welcome visitors, though many do. In a couple of schools in particular, the principals were constantly solicited, but managed to carve an hour for our interview, during which we were interrupted several times. Many of the teachers whose classes I observed had no idea I was coming until I showed up at their classroom door. All schools, their teachers, staff, and students were welcoming and open. And other than the specific character of the schools as Muslim schools, which I detail later, I could have been in any French school.

Notes

1. https://www.al-kanz.org/2014/10/11/enseignement-prive-musulman/.
2. http://www.desdomesetdesminarets.fr/2017/06/05/85-ecoles-et-projets-decoles-privees-musulmanes-en-france-la-liste-complete/et; https://www.imanemagazine.com/ecole-college-lycee-musulman/.
3. https://www.francetvinfo.fr/replay-radio/le-vrai-du-faux/le-vrai-du-faux-oui-le-nombre-d-ecoles-musulmanes-augmente-en-france-mais-dans-les-memes-proportions-que-les-autres-etablissements_2811681.html.
4. http://educactive.com/reglement-interieur-au-lycee/.

References

Krempf, Antoine. « Le vrai du faux. Oui, le nombre d'écoles musulmanes augmente en France, mais dans les mêmes proportions que les autres établissements. » franceinfo: *Radio France*, 5 July 2018. https://www.francetvinfo.fr/replay-radio/le-vrai-du-faux/le-vrai-du-faux-oui-le-nombre-d-ecoles-musulmanes-augmente-en-france-mais-dans-les-memes-proportions-que-les-autres-etablissements_2811681.html.

Poucet, Bruno. *L'enseignement privé en France*. Paris: PUF, 2012.

Poucet, Bruno. « La naissance d'une école privée musulmane sous contrat ? » *L'Etat et l'enseignement privé : L'application de la loi Debré*. Ed. Bruno Poucet. Rennes: Presses universitaires de Rennes, 2011. 263–275.

CHAPTER 3

Islamic Schools Successes: Averroes and Al-Kindi

Averroès

Averroes is located in a working-class neighborhood right at the outskirt of the northern city of Lille, within very easy reach through public transportation. I spent two days there in late September 2016. I first met with the principal, who had been at his post for a dozen years. Over the course of those couple of days, I met formally and informally with the principal, the assistant principals, the president of the FNEM (Makhlouf Mamèche), several teachers over breaks in the teachers' lounge, in the cafeteria, and in the public bus, and attended Arabic and Religion classes (Picture 3.1).

History

The genesis for this high school is clearly stated on the website. After the 1994 exclusion of about twenty veiled girls from the Faidherbe high school, at the height of the second moment in the affair of the scarf, the Islamic League of the North, a local association founded in 1983, took charge of their education by registering them for distance education and setting up a support system in the Al Imane mosque in the southern suburb of the city. Thus, the idea of founding a school was born out of a pressing need. This experience spurred the creation of the high school, but it took time to collect donations and set up the project. Averroes High School opened its door in 2003 with fifteen students.

Picture 3.1 Lycée Averroès, Lille, September 2016

Its enrolment was 463 students in 2013 when I first started working on this project, with an extensive waiting list. A middle school was added in 2012. In Fall 2016, they welcomed a total of about 820 students, which probably made Averroès the largest Muslim school.

Mission, Curriculum, and Religious Character

The curriculum follows the national curriculum, it also includes Arabic language and an optional Muslim Ethics course. According to the principal, Averroès will not expand beyond middle and high school, because they prefer to consolidate what they have done so far. They have four classes per grade at the middle school, and five per grade at the high school. The high school offers all three general studies tracks: L (Literary studies), S (Scientific studies), E (Economics/social sciences) plus one technological track in Management (STMG). Students benefit from individualized follow-up to ensure their success.

The high school's mission, in addition to quality education, is to help students reconcile their dual identity and to live their being French and Muslim in harmony. They stress to parents the "religious and spiritual environment and training that will allow their children to live harmoniously their dual French and Muslim identity."[1] The name of Averroès (Ibn Rushd in Arabic) was chosen because he is the "best symbol to illustrate a fruitful encounter between Islam and Europe," and a "reference for anyone who claims this dual belonging" (https://www.lycee-averroes.com).

The Muslim character of the school is its "added value," and the pedagogical project is inspired by the following (Muslim) values: "the search for perfection, a liking for effort, love of knowledge, a sense of engagement and sharing, an open mind and respect for others" (website). The school is open to all, and views itself as an example of "the necessary bridge between Muslim spirituality and French society." Its specific character as a confessional school can be seen through fostering "universal values of solidarity, fraternity, and sharing" (https://www.lycee-averroes.com). There is a prayer room for those who wish to pray during breaks, but most students do not make use of it (Bras et al. 47). When I was there, I saw a handful of teachers and students pray one afternoon. Friday is the only day when the school organizes a collective prayer led by the ethics teacher who delivers the sermon. There is no dress code, but they do forbid garments such as torn jeans that are in fashion. The school was recently expanded with an additional building and facilities are still in the process of being renovated. They have a spacious cafeteria serving halal meals; it was still decorated for the Eid that had just been celebrated a couple of weeks before my visit.

Contract and Budget

Averroès signed a contract with the state in 2008, five years after its opening. In an interview with a newspaper, the director of the school is quoted as saying that it was not easy to get the contract, because the

Rectorat did not want to take the decision. In the end, the Ministry of Education gave the agreement (cited in Mahuzier). This is an example of how schools can be at the mercy of local authorities. This seems to limit what Bras et al. stated in their report, that the strong presence and role of the Catholic University in Lille paved the way for Muslim institutions to grow (52). Opening a school requires approval at many levels of local authorities (city, department, academy), and sometimes opposition at one level is all it takes to completely sabotage a project, as we will see in the next chapter. According to Makhlouf Mamèche, Averroes was lucky to get all its high school classes under contract at once, since then the policy has been to contract one class at a time.

The school always does fundraising. The high school does balance its budget, all classes are under contract and the regional authorities are quite generous for private schools, therefore Averroès gets a high percentage of administrative expenses (secretarial support, principal, monitors) covered. However, the middle school (too recent to be under contract) carried a big deficit when we spoke in 2016.

Student Selection and Demographics

Students are selected based on an application that includes the following: grades, behavior, and an interview with parents to make sure that they support the school's project: their view of Islam in society, the role of education (for instance supporting girls' careers), co-ed, no restrictions in the subjects studied. They end up having more girls than boys because girls have better grades and behavior (Interview September 2016). All socioeconomic levels are represented in the school, but they have a high percentage of students who get need-based scholarships from the Ministry of Education (60%), which is much higher than the average for private schools (around 11% according to the director).[2]

Most students spring from immigration from the Maghreb. There are children of Salafists in the school and different rites but everybody keeps their faith for themselves (Interview September 2016). They also have a few non-Muslim students, some from mixed families who are not religious. They also have two students from non-Muslim families who chose Averroes because it is private, close to their home, and they are used to dealing with Muslims; one of them even attends the optional ethics class.

Teachers

The school is able to select the teachers that are under contract with the state, and while most of the teachers are Muslim, they have at least 6 or 7 who are not. There are about 80 teachers at Averroes; they have an association to do things such as buy a coffee machine, help teachers with the national exams, and give input on life at school. One Arabic teacher praised the good atmosphere of the school, and the support from colleagues and parents. One of the administrators who has worked many years in Catholic schoolsprior to joining Averroès sees no difference between Averroes and Catholic schools other than the special character which is Catholic for one and Muslim for the other. One exception is the staff's commitment: teachers give more of their time, they have a sense of duty to maintain the success of the school. He also felt that the Zitouni affair had strengthened the bond between the team of teachers and administrators.

Extra-Curricular Activities and Field Trips

There are miscellaneous activities, including lectures by scholars of Islam and interfaith dialog, workshops about higher education tracks, and other topics such as the media offered by a former editor of *Le Monde*, and one week of humanitarian solidarity awareness. Religious events seem to be a minority (mawlid celebration in January 2014, *iftar* or fast-breaking meal during Ramadan with a teacher in June 2016).

The website showcased bits about various field trips. For instance, 11th graders went to Paris to watch a performance of the famous play *Cyrano de Bergerac* which was on the program for the baccalauréat (national high school exam) that they were taking at the end of the school year, in the theater. Other fieldtrips took students to Agadir, Istanbul, and on a ski trip (https://www.lycee-averroes.com). The website also highlighted various students' achievements. One student qualified for the national final of the dictée francophone 2016 (roughly equivalent to a spelling bee). A picture of the 2014 graduating class shows 10 girls and 7 boys in American style graduation attire.

Engagement with current events includes notes condemning the attacks against Charlie Hebdo with a minute of silence observed by the school, and reactions to the attacks in Paris in November 2015, with the school canceling classes in solidarity with the victims. A memo from the principal categorically condemning these and all terrorist attacks, and deploring the fact that Islam and its values "had been betrayed and tarnished" was posted on 7 January 2015.[3]

Success

An important measure of Averroès' success is to have been named best high school in France in 2013, a mere ten years after its opening, ahead of traditional power houses such as Lycées Louis Legrand and Henri IV (the Ivy League of French high schools). Every year, the Ministry of Education releases data about the success of students at the national baccalauréat (bac) exam for all French high schools; various newspapers then rank high schools based on these numbers. Based on the 2012 data, Averroes high school was ranked number 1 by *Le Parisien* and *Le point*, number 5 by *L'Express* and number 2 by *Le monde* (out of almost 2000 schools), thanks to its 100% success in the bac but also because children who enter the school in 10th grade have a 99% chance of obtaining their diploma. Averroès subsequently added a middle school, which seems to be doing as well as the high school according to a Facebook post in July 2017 that congratulated the performance of students for the middle school exam: 98.8% success rate (only one out of 81 students failed), 80% with honors (mention), 55% with high honors (mentions bien ou très bien).

When I asked the director what he thought made the success of the school, he mentioned that eight out of ten members of the administrative council are or were members of the National Education, that the community was very supportive, and that it had a charismatic leader in the person of Amar Lasfar; all these factors contributed to the material conditions needed for success. In addition, as director he does not deal with budget issues (it is the responsibility of the school board), contrary to other schools where directors have to worry about paying the teachers. Moreover, the individual follow-up, strict school rules and required involvement from parents are crucial for students' academic success.

The number of students per class is relatively high compared to other private schools, with a cap at 30 for middle school and 35 in the high school. Nevertheless, they have such a long waiting list in particular for the middle school grades, that they could open three middle schools. They have three requests per two spots in the high school, and between five and six for two spots in the middle school. He explained that by qualifying middle schools as the weak link of the public school system, particularly 8th grade.

Controversy

Averroès made national headlines again in 2016, but this time, it was not great news: its philosophy teacher, Sofiane Zitouni, resigned after teaching for five months only in a very public way by publishing an op-ed in one of the national newspapers, accusing the school of harassment (after he published a piece stating that "The Prophet is also Charlie" following the attacks on Charlie Hebdo), students of rampant antisemitism, and the school direction and teachers of a double discourse hiding an Islamist political agenda ("Pourquoi"). One of Averroes ethics' teachers wrote a rebuttal (Meziani). Zitouni later on expanded on his few months at Averroes and the backlash he experienced after associating the Prophet of Islam with the newspaper that defiled him in a chapter titled "The high school which was Averroes in name only" (*Confessions*).[4] In addition to what was already in his op-ed, he explained that the UOIF's alliance with political parties of the right have helped to deliver a Muslim vote to the right to gain cities that were traditionally voting to the left, in exchange for the contract. He points out the role played by Michel Soussan, former inspector from the academy, pedagogical counselor for the school, and right-wing city council member.[5]

The school staff were stunned by the accusations (Deffresnnes). The Rectorat sent a special mission to inspect the school following Zitouni's allegations, but did not find any violation. The school sued Zitouni for libel. Zitouni was first condemned, but won his appeal. Carol Ferrara, an American student in Anthropology who was conducting research for her dissertation and spent time at Averroes, wrote a piece that presented itself as an "objective and neutral perspective" as a non-Muslim, non-French who had spent two weeks at Averroes observing classes, interviewing teachers and students ("Mes observations"). She disputed the double talk alleged by Zitouni, and commented: "It is true that the discourse on Islam at the high school is close to the UOIF and its president Amar Lasfar, as Mr. Zitouni noticed; but, given my knowledge, experiences, and perspectives, I do not see this discourse as a threat against France" ("Mes observations"). When the issue came up in the teachers' lounge during my visit, several people (including one non-Muslim teacher) said that Ferrara's piece was a fair one. The philosophy teacher who took over after Zitouni's resignation also wrote a piece to support Averroes as a non-Muslim who was 100% behind Averroes. He wrote that he had to work hard with students to help them catch up because Zitouni had been talking more about religion in class instead of focusing on philosophy (Urani). This is somewhat corroborated by Zitouni himself, since in his book he mentions making many references to Islam during his philosophy classes and justifying this by the fact that this was a Muslim school.

Arabic

Arabic is offered as first (LVI), second (LVII), and third (LVIII) foreign language. Students do not have to study Arabic in the high school, where it is offered as a foreign language like all others. It is compulsory in 6th and 7th grade only, and that year, only 18 students chose to pursue Arabic beyond 7th grade, which was a surprisingly low number for me. Teachers follow the curriculum established by the Ministry of Education, which the principal thinks lags behind compared to other languages because Arabic studies were considered for Arabs and devalued. Other languages offered are English as LVI, and German and Spanish as LVII. Arabic is taught with English starting in the sixth grade.

One Arabic teacher has an MA in Arabic and was teaching at Averroes for the second year, the other was in her second year for her MA degree. This was the first batch of students who started in 6th grade and were reaching a B2 level in 12th grade. A majority of students have dialectal Arabic at home. Families tend to favor other languages that are taught in the *grandes écoles* (elite higher education schools). One teacher mentioned that she had been inspected twice already even though the norm is once every five years. They took 30 students to Agadir in Morocco in the context of Arabic classes.

Religion

A report published in 2010 explains that Hassan Iquioussen, member of the UOIF and founder of an association under its umbrella, Muslim Youth of France (Jeunes musulmans de France), was first tasked with the religious ethics class. When the current director started, he replaced Iquioussen because of a lack of curriculum and frequent absences in 2008, only to have the same problem regarding absenteeism. At the time of the report, a doctoral student in sociology at the EHESS, was in charge of the class, which was planned as a history of Islam (Bras et al.). According to the director, the religion class faces the following difficulties: high school students do not really have time to dedicate to the teaching of religion because all their focus is on the high school exam. Moreover, the lack of curriculum stems from the need for Muslims to think long term. According to the report, he believes that ethics should be addressed transversally, through teachers' attitude (rigor, punctuality) as well as the values transmitted to students. Most students did not take the ethics class, which is not graded. The director underlined the difficulty to find properly trained teachers for Arabic and Muslim ethics (Bras et al. 47), something which has been echoed to me in other schools.

The ethics class is described as a "teaching that integrates contemporary issues" (website); its duration is one hour and a half weekly from middle to high school. All students except one take it at the middle school, as well as all students in the 10th grade, but fewer in 11th and 12th grades. According to the principal, the course should give a stimulating vision of Islam to integrate in society as a citizen. The administration trusts the teachers who have the freedom to do what they want within these broad guidelines. The class should not revolve exclusively around Islam, especially not the dichotomy of haram/halal. There are three teachers teaching the ethics class, which becomes a Muslim civilization class in 12th grade.

During my visit, I got to meet two ethics teachers. During a brief conversation, one teacher explained that her classes emphasize behavior, respect of others, universal values at the middle school level, and more complex issues at the high school level. The second teacher, who had been teaching ethics at Averroes full time for four years, had the time to grant me an interview. He studied philosophy before spending a year of intensive studies at the renowned al-Azhar university in Cairo. According to him, the main goal of a Muslim school is to graduate high school students who are prepared to succeed in higher education, with a serene understanding of their faith, and blooming citizens. His objective for middle school is to give basic notions through stories. In 6th grade, they start with the five pillars, and basic history through stories from the companions. Students generally have many questions related to teenagehood and to relationships with their peers and adults, so he tries to talk about Islam from their real-life issues. In the middle school (which includes 9th grade in France), he sees a lot of doubt about faith, the existence of God, and his class is an opportunity for them to ask questions they might not dare ask elsewhere. He starts some basic exegesis with the 9th graders and goes more in depth in high school.

In high school, they look at deep questions, as well as current issues. This teacher's goal is to arouse a maximum of questions and give a minimum of responses. In 11th grade, they focus on Islamic ethics, and distinguish between ethics and morals to lead students to answer the following question: how should I live my life? He gives them a dilemma about how to weigh things, for instance, between wearing the veil and the duty to learn. He does not give ready-made answers but elements to lead them to answer the questions by themselves. He hopes to deliver students from a traditional interpretation of Islam, to filter the essence from the culture, to cultivate critical thinking, and to return to the basics of Islamic ethics that are responsibility and free will. In 12th grade, they tackle Muslim philosophy. What he sees as the main difficulty for students is that they get most of their references from the Internet, which makes it hard to have an intellectual conversation; the other difficulty is to fight some of their misunderstanding of Islam (various superstitions that they can't seem to shake off). He gets lots of questions in the high school about various conspiracy theories and other simplistic explanations to analyze the world, because students watch all kinds of things on the Internet. Other favorite topics include the representation of Islam in the media, and relationships between boys and girls. In addition to the optional class, they offer workshops, including some targeted for girls and for boys separately about sexuality.

Al Kindi

History

The opening of Al Kindi caused some controversy because of the opposition of the rector of the Lyon academy, Alain Morvan. Bras et al. recall that there were historical tensions at play between strong secular proponents and strong Catholic supporters in the Lyon area, and that the addition of Islam to the religious landscape had been a source of more conflicts there than elsewhere, with events such as the founding of the UJM and Tariq Ramadan's role in it, Khaled Kelkal, and the mayor of Vénissieux sponsoring the law on the niqab (52). Whether these were

Picture 3.2 Poster on the wall, Al-Kindi, Décines-Charpieu, September 2016. The quote translates literally as: "To have done more for the world than the world has done for you: that is success," a slight mistranslation of Ford's "to do for the world more than the world does for you--that is success"

factors that played or not, the opening of the school was delayed by one of three required state representative authorizations (Picture 3.2).

Bassiouni details the events: Morvan opposed the opening of the school three times, even though the mayor and the préfet granted their approval. First, the building was not adequate. The people responsible for the project, Hakim Chergui and Nizar Hakim, changed the location of the school to address those concerns, only to have it rejected again, with two main justifications: ground pollution and the fact that the planned director for the school was already a full-time teacher and that he would not be on a one-year leave as planned to direct the new school. Local Muslim associations mobilized and organized demonstrations, and the third rejection was overturned on appeal. Morvan was then dismissed as rector for opposing Al Kindi.

Morvan later on related his experience in his book *L'honneur et les honneurs*, in which he first insists on polluted soil and other safety issues as his main reasons. He explains that pressure was put on the Ministry of education by the Ministry of Interior (led by Sarkozy, candidate for the presidential elections, looking for votes) to approve Al Kindi no matter what, which leads Morvan to dramatize the situation as "un complot contre la République" "a plot against the Republic" (211). Bassiouni notes the strong ties established between the local and regional Muslim associations and the Catholic Church whose representatives lent support for the project, the role played by the affiliation of the people carrying the project with the UOIF[6] whose image in the public is very negative, and the politicization of the whole affair by Morvan himself, who associated fundamentalism and *communautarisme* with the project and the people carrying it when speaking to the media.

Al Kindi eventually opened in March 2007 with one 6th grade class of 16 students. It grew very quickly and became the first private K-12 Muslim school, encompassing elementary, middle, and high schools together under one roof. In 2013, it claimed it was the largest private Muslim school and grew as follows:

2007–2008: 7 classes from 6th to 10th grade.
2008–2009: 243 students in 14 classes from 6th to 11th grade.
2009–2010: 20 classes from 6th to 12th with 343 students.
2010–2011: it opened the elementary school and reached
            450 students.
2013–2014: 480 students.

In 2016, they had 525 students, with 2 sections of grades 6–10, 4 classes of 11th grade (sections L & ES grouped together), and 3 sections of 12th grade. The elementary school had 121 students in five classes, one each per grade from 1 to 5. The elementary grades are capped at 25 students maximum per class, the middle school ones at 30.

Al Kindi is located in Descines-Charpieu, a suburb of Lyon within easy reach through public transportation. It borders Vaux-en-Velin (notorious for riots that erupted there in 1990), the third poorest town in France.[7] I visited Al Kindi in September 2016. It has separate directors for the primary and secondary grades. I met the director for the middle and high school, who is originally from Algeria. Al Kindi has spacious buildings, playgrounds, a cafeteria, a music room, a computer room, and a lab. The director emphasized that they do invest in the facilities even though they are temporary.

Mission, Curriculum, and Religious Character

Self-described as a school with a Muslim reference, Al Kindi stresses on its website that it is open to all regardless of faith, and aims for excellence and quality teaching in an ethical environment that respects Muslim values. Al Kindi's first vocation is to foster academic excellence and knowledge according to Muslim ethics and values, taking the whole person into account while being open to the world. All grades follow the national curriculum. The high school offers all three general studies tracks (ES, S, L), plus STMG. The school moto is "Héritage, Endurance et Succès," with an emphasis on endurance because it is the key to success. Their educational project insists on being open to the world and forming well-rounded students, and aims for spiritual and citizenly success (http://www.al-kindi.fr 2013). The director emphasized the project of the school to help students build an identity as "Républicains qui sont fiers de ce qu'ils sont" "citizens of the French Republic proud of who they are" and who would be the first to defend their country because of their faith. The school makes a point of emphasizing our common humanity.

The choice of name is explained by telling a tidbit about Al Kindi, whose full name was Yaqoub Ibn Ishâq Al Kindi (801–873), and who is presented as the first Arab philosopher and as a model to be followed to show the younger generations the depth of their heritage, and how to combine science with spirituality (http://www.al-kindi.fr 2016). While we were touring the school, we ran into a former student who had just returned from a one-year trip to China. She came to her former school to donate some books, and to suggest offering a workshop about Asian countries. After she left, the principal praised and held her as a sign of the school's success; he wants his students to be a diamond for France, because he loves the country and is a believer.

The school does not have a uniform, but has a dress code that forbids training pants (except for PE classes). The scarf is not compulsory. There is no class on Friday afternoon to allow students to attend the weekly prayer.

Contract and Budget

The school began receiving partial subvention from a contract with the state in 2012 for 6th and 10th grades only. According to its website, state subsidies provided 6.7% of the total budget, tuition 38% (http://www.al-kindi.fr 2013). Fundraising fills the gap, and sometimes in-kind donations (some equipment was donated by companies).

Al Kindi had a unique tuition scale based on families' income; for 2016, for taxable incomes above 50,000 euros, maximum tuition was 2500 for all levels, and tuition varied between 1400 and 1700 for incomes under 9500 euros.

Student Selection and Demographics

Criteria for admission is detailed as follows on the website: grades, behavior, motivation of the student and the family, siblings, geographical distance, and availability. After evaluation of the file, there is an interview of children and parents together to make sure that they are a good fit, to evaluate motivations, to present the schools' educational project, and to answer any questions (http://www.al-kindi.fr 2016). The main criterion for admission is the parents' commitment and willingness to be involved in the school (Interview 2016). The director receives admission requests year round. Priority is given to veiled girls because they have nowhere else to go, so the veil is a factor but it is not the only one. Other factors are taken into account, such as siblings attending the school.

According to the director, all socioeconomic levels are represented (he recently had the case of a 17-year-old homeless student), as well as more than 17 nationalities. There are many different backgrounds, including Muslim, mixed marriages, non-practicing, but the common motivation for all families is the quality of education. He insisted that this is not a madrasa or theological school. There is roughly an equal number of boys and girls, though in the high school the ES section has 7 girls and 4 boys for a total of 11.

Teachers

There is a variety of background, with some having passed the competitive national exam (concours) to be a teacher, others in the process of doing so, or having equivalents such as the CAPES from Tunisia. Some have CDI (temporary) contracts. The director expressed the hope to have more than 30% of tenured (titulaire) teachers soon, which would bring more stability to the school. There are non-Muslim teachers. In a private conversation, one teacher praised the teaching staff at Al Kindi and described it as a united team of forty-something that believes in the project of the school.

Extra-Curricular Activities and Field Trips

The website has a header for "Activités culturelles et sportives" "Cultural and Athletic activities" which are organized in order to develop well-rounded personalities (opening to the world, develop general knowledge, critical thinking and creativity), but no sport is mentioned.

Here is a glimpse of what was offered in 2015:

- Café philo at lunch time once a week organized by the philosophy teacher, open to all high school students to initiate students to philosophical thinking on various topics.
- Conferences and workshops on civic and religious education on issues relevant to the youth and their relationship with society and religion, organized by several teachers for 8–12 grades.
- Workshop on Muslim civilization to initiate students to this heritage. The website mentions specifically the fact this is meant to fill a gap because history textbooks barely mention Muslim civilization. It is organized by the history and geography teacher and gives an overview of the main Muslim dynasties.
- Workshop on the prophet's life, offered by the religion teacher to look at the prophet's life and draw analogies with our time and wisdom from various events of his life.

In addition to cultural activities, another category labeled "Activités Spirituelles et Citoyennes" "Spiritual and citizenly activities" is offered, although it might be difficult to draw a clear line between the two:

- Workshops twice a week on "Tajwid" (rules for recitation of the Qur'an)
- In 2015–2016, activities were organized around the question "what does engagement mean for a Muslim?" with a conference given by a lawyer

- Workshops to sensitize students to various humanitarian crises around the world, through events such as a solidarity race for Senegal in 2013, one for Gaza in collaboration with an NGO, and one for Syria as a fundraiser for an NGO.

Field Trips

Ice breaker weekends are organized for the middle and high schools at the beginning of the school year in the Alps for hiking. Fourth and fifth graders were taken on a three-day field trip in the countryside for an environmental and rural geography theme.

Success

In 2012, the middle school students had a national exam pass rate of 90%, and the high school 93% success at the baccalauréat (with 100% in the ES and STMG tracks). In 2010, Al Kindi was reported to receive 1000 applications a year (Bras et al. 35). In 2016, they had to turn down about 500 applications (Interview 2016).

Arabic

In the elementary school, students get 4 hours of Arabic a week; the school also offers Turkish for students who speak it at home. In the middle school, students start with Arabic language and English in 6th grade. The main challenge is the wide range of levels for Arabic among students, each class is split into 2 groups of different levels, but there are not enough teachers for all. Other foreign languages include English, Spanish (and German through distance classes). English is compulsory as first language (LVI), Arabic compulsory as second or third (LVII or III). For the teaching of Arabic, one teacher noted that there are challenges that need to be overcome in terms of organization, coherence, and continuity (there is no continuity between primary and secondary, students go from 4 hours in elementary to 2 hours in 6th grade). Most students do not have Arabic at home, they are second and third generation so their parents do not speak Arabic, sometimes the grandparents speak it a little (or Berber).

Religion

There is an optional hour of Islamic culture and ethics class that includes a discovery of other religions and spiritualities. The director laments the fact that there is no program for religion classes, but in general, the guideline is to focus on universal values and not on the various practices and polemical topics. The class is called "Éveil à la foi" "Spiritual Awakening" in the elementary grades. Only two students from the elementary school do not attend the class, which he interprets as a sign that parents do see a benefit in it. The school is currently in the process of revising its curriculum for the "Culture of Islam" course at the middle school. His vision for the religion classes is to develop a spiritual awakening, an understanding about the cultures of Islam to provide a foundation to put Islam in dialogue. He insisted that there is no constraint in faith, on the simplicity of Islam and that one should not complicate matters further. He stressed the importance of knowledge for Islam, reminding me that the first revealed verse of the Qur'an was an injunction to read.

Religion classes at the secondary school are split between 2 teachers: one is a specialist of Pakistani Islamic culture, who has been teaching at Al Kindi for two years full-time, teaches all classes in middle school as well as 10th graders. He is not interested in fiqh because he feels students are "polluted" by that, focusing on questions of haram/halal (what is forbidden/allowed) is not interesting for him, as it makes us forget intellectual dynamics. He wants to build an interesting program for the long term. The other teacher is the rector (administrator) of a nearby mosque, and a science teacher in another institution. He has established a program for the last two years of high school that focuses on understanding the texts in the context in which one lives, to push students to think about their place as Muslims in France.

Notes

1. https://www.lycee-averroes.com/.
2. The website emphasizes this fact as well and gives roughly the same numbers. http://www.fnem.fr/le-lycee-musulman-averroes-un-symbole-au-coeur-de-la-polemique/.
3. « L'horreur, ce mercredi 7 janvier à Charlie Hebdo.

> En ces heures de deuil national, nous tenons d'abord à présenter nos sincères condoléances aux familles et aux proches des victimes ainsi qu'à l'ensemble des salariés de Charlie Hebdo.
> Nous partageons le sentiment national de stupeur devant cet acte de barbarie.
> Nous condamnons de la manière la plus ferme cet attentat terroriste.
> À travers cet acte odieux ce sont l'islam et ses valeurs qui ont été trahis et souillés.
> Une minute de silence sera observée au lycée à 12h00. »
> Directeur Lycée collège AVERROÈS, communiqué 7 janvier 2015.

4. For a counterpoint, see Eric Dufour's reaction to Zitouni's book.
5. Michel Soussan was inspector of the Northern Academy, and the founders of Averroes contacted him when girls were expelled from Faidherbe. Soussan suggested they open a Muslim school. As inspector, he wrote a positive report on Averroes in 2004. There was resistance from the Rectorat and Ministry who were fine with the 10th grade classes going under contract, but eventually, the whole high school was approved. Soussan has the formal title of pedagogical adviser at Averroes, he stayed on to help the director, do teacher training, and work with parents (He mentioned his internet site for his consulting company). He is also on the city council of Lille, and also has positions at the department level. He stays with Averroes for the symbol, to support it, as this was the time when the lawsuit against the newspaper *Libération* was going to court. In several articles, he is cited as categorically denying the allegations of antisemitism against Averroes. He arranged his nephew's visit, a rabbi, for an interfaith dialogue moderated by Zitouni (available at https://www.youtube.com/watch?v=ZDii7fKk73s). While Zitouni recounts in his book that students had been told by the school direction not to talk about the Israeli–Palestinian conflict, the ethics teacher dived right into the issue during this event.
6. Nazir Hakim, president of the Al Kindi association proposing the school, was Vice President of the UOIF, and Azzedine Gaci, a member of the committee created for support, was one of the local UOIF representatives.
7. https://www.nouvelobs.com/societe/20151002.AFP1672/retour-sur-vaulx-en-velin-25-ans-apres-les-emeutes-une-ville-en-renouveau-des-habitants-fragiles.html.

References

Bassiouni, Moustapha Chérif. « La naissance du collège-lycée Al-Kindi à Décines: une réussite conflictuelle. » *L'Année du Maghreb* IV (2008): 401–421. http://journals.openedition.org/anneemaghreb/468; https://doi.org/10.4000/anneemaghreb.468.

Bras, J.-P., S. Mervin, S. Amghar, L. Fournier, O. Marongiu, and B. Godard. "L'enseignement de l'Islam dans les écoles coraniques les institutions de formation islamique et les écoles privées." Rapport du IISMM & EHESS, 2010. http://www.disons.fr/wp-content/uploads/2012/03/RAPPORTENSEIGNEMENT-ISLAMIQUE-final.pdf.

Deffrennes, Geoffroy « Stupéfaction au lycée musulman Averroès après des accusations d'intégrisme. » *Le Monde.fr*, 7 February 2015. https://www.lemonde.fr/education/article/2015/02/07/stupefaction-au-lycee-musulman-averroes-apres-des-accusations-d-integrisme_4571957_1473685.html.

Dufour, Éric. « J'ai mal à ma France: de la misislamie ou la République face à elle-même. » *SaphirNews*, 19 Avril 2016. https://www.saphirnews.com/J-ai-mal-a-ma-France-de-la-misislamie-ou-la-Republique-face-a-elle-meme_a22263.html.

Ferrara, Carol. « Mes observations en tant que chercheuse au sein du lycée Averroès. » *SaphirNews*, 14 Février 2015. https://www.saphirnews.com/Mes-observations-en-tant-que-chercheuse-au-sein-du-lycee-Averroes_a20410.html.

Mahuzier, Marc. « À Lille, le seul lycée privé musulman sous contrat. » *Ouest France*.

Meziani, Sofiane. « "Charlie Hebdo": le problème n'est pas religieux. Stigmatiser les musulmans est une erreur. » *L'Obs le Plus*, 20 January 2015. http://leplus.nouvelobs.com/contribution/1309232-charlie-hebdo-le-probleme-n-est-pas-religieux-stigmatiser-les-musulmans-est-une-erreur.html.

Morvan, Alain. *L'honneur et les honneurs: souvenirs d'un recteur kärchérisé*. Paris: Grasset, 2008.

No author. « RETOUR SUR – Vaulx-en-Velin: 25 ans après les émeutes, une ville en renouveau, des habitants fragiles. » *L'Obs*, 2 octobre 2015. https://www.nouvelobs.com/societe/20151002.AFP1672/retour-sur-vaulx-en-velin-25-ans-apres-les-emeutes-une-ville-en-renouveau-des-habitants-fragiles.html.

Urani, Stéphen. « Pourquoi je reviens au lycée Averroès. » *SaphirNews*, 17 Février 2015. https://www.saphirnews.com/Pourquoi-je-reviens-au-lycee-Averroes_a20440.html.

Zitouni, Soufiane. « Pourquoi j'ai démissionné du lycée Averroès. » *Libération*, 5 février 2015. http://www.liberation.fr/societe/2015/02/05/pourquoi-j-ai-demissionne-du-lycee-averroes_1196424.

Zitouni, Soufiane. « Un lycée qui n'avait d'Averroès que le nom. » *Confessions d'un fils de Marianne et de Mahomet*. Paris: Les Echappés, 2016. 221–240.

CHAPTER 4

Islamic Schools Challenges: Réussite and IFSQY/Samarcande

Part I: Réussite

Unfortunately, I was unable to visit Réussite while it was open, but I am nevertheless including it in this study for two reasons. First, it shares with La Plume the label of being the very first Muslim school in France, and it is without a doubt the very first Muslim middle school in France, the first Muslim school in the Parisian area and the first in the department of Seine-Saint-Denis. Second, it also stands out by the level of hurdles it has encountered in its application to get a contract with the State. It gives particular insight into the difficulties that some Muslim schools can face, and how local and national politics, but also individuals can affect various outcomes.

After emails and phone calls to request an interview and school visit went unanswered, I showed up at the school twice in September 2016, only to be gently turned away by the receptionist who assured me that she would pass on my coordinates and a copy of my first book to the director who was unavailable. I never heard back. I had more luck the second time around when Dhaou Meskine himself picked up the phone in 2018. He was never notified by the receptionist, and eagerly agreed to an interview conducted in March 2018 at the school's facilities, with a follow-up in June 2018.

The following section draws information from this interview as well as from other sources. First, the school website which I first consulted in 2013 when I started working on this project, then in 2016 before my

© The Author(s) 2019
C. Bourget, *Islamic Schools in France*,
https://doi.org/10.1007/978-3-030-03834-2_4

first round of visits to schools. When I looked for it again in 2018, it had been taken down following the closure of the school in 2017. There are a few videos that were taped at the school; unfortunately, some of them are no longer available. Another important source of information is John Bowen's landmark study, where he recounts several opportunities to observe and participate in the school and association's activities in the early 2000s.

History

The first private junior high Muslim school was opened in September 2001 by the association Réussite, which had been doing after-school tutoring for 9 years. Jack Ralite, mayor of Aubervilliers from 1984 to 2003, needed votes for his reelection; therefore, he facilitated the permit to open the school, though not without trying to dissuade Meskine from doing so (Interview March 2018). Meskine went ahead anyways because he thought it was in the best interest of the French Republic to open such a school (Interview March 2018). The non-profit organization also offered Qur'an and Arabic classes and summer camps, with the goal of helping students to succeed. The school was located in the city of Aubervilliers in the Seine-St-Denis, which is a department that has been traditionally working class and that is notorious for its failed housing policies that have created ghettos of immigrants. This is also the department in which the 2005 riots first erupted.[1] Yet, as John Bowen sarcastically points out, Aubervilliers "is not grim, not isolated, and not 'communalist,' the favorite slap-down of central Paris intellectuals for the suburbs they never see. It is as ethnically mixed a place as you could find in France" (111).

The school building is a lot more spacious than the entrance leads one to believe, with a science lab, a computer lab, classrooms and offices, an inside courtyard with basketball hoops (which one would never guess was there from the outside), a multi-purpose hall, and two rooms that served as cafeterias (one for girls and one for boys).

As Bowen pointed out, at its peak, "The Success School is a multidimensional space, all Muslim ambiance but offering a regular day school curriculum, night classes for adults in Arabic, after-school and weekend tutoring and courses for children, and weekend vacations and summer family camp. Dhaou Meskine holds all this together […] Dhaou is at the center of a network of institutions and activities that include, in addition to the school, his imam duties in Clichy-sous-bois, the institute we read of in chapter five, his position as the secretary-general of the national Council of Imams, and his role managing two properties in Normandy, which he is building into permanent sites for weekend and summer activities" (2010: 112). Meskine was clearly the driving force leading many different activities, all geared toward the Muslim community in France. He had started a private school in his native Tunisia that followed the national curriculum but provided a Muslim environment, kind of a precursor to the school he would later on found in France (Bowen 2010: 112–113). Bowen quotes him explaining that he had not intended to start a Muslim school, but to help Muslim students succeed in an area notorious for school failure. John Bowen spent time shadowing Meskine, and reported on Meskine's various roles in his book, as imam (Bowen 38) and educator in various settings (Bowen 2010: 112–114).

Three registered associations were set up in 2003 for each activity: Réussite Teaching for the school and after-school tutoring, Réussite Culture for the Arabic Language courses, and Réussite Leasures for the camps and outings (Bowen 2010: 125–126). According to Bowen, both the school and family camp were "an attempt to build an institution with a secular set of activities and universalist goals (training, recreation, introduction to rural France) that yet preserves an Islamic ambiance. This is religion outside the narrow French official definition: religion suffusing everyday life. If the religion in question is Catholic, it is part of the French heritage. Will France accept it if it is a religion that had been thought of until recently as alien?" (2010: 128–129).

Meskine kept wearing many hats over the years. In addition to being remunerated as director of the association that oversees the school, he taught Arabic, led the association Leasures, was part of the Imams Council, and also part of the Muslim Association of the 93 department. He has also been involved in interfaith dialogue: for instance, he was the first one to issue a fatwa condemning the murder of the Tibhirine monks, and Réussite loaned its school bus to a Jewish school whose bus had burnt (Interview March 2018).

School in Session 2001–2017

The first class opened in 2001 with 11 students in 6th grade. In a news segment on several Muslim schools taped by the TV channel France 24 that aired in 2010, Réussite had 130 students from 6th to 11th grade (the 11th grade class was the scientific track).[2] A section filmed in class shows more than 20 students in the classroom. The religious education teacher explains that he teaches the basics of Islam in an optional class one hour a week. A 6th grade girl says she wanted to come to this school because she can wear her headscarf and pray. The reporter highlights that the main goal of the school is success, achieved thanks to small class sizes. In another video, students mention the advantage of being able to practice their religion inside the school (praying, reading Qur'an). The video highlights the 100% pass rate at the Bac.[3]

Mission, Curriculum, and Religious Character

The Réussite followed the national curriculum, but added extra math and French classes, offered Arabic and English as LV1 in 6th grade, and one optional hour of religious education per week. For the high school, they had the scientific track because of parents' demands, though Meskine himself would have preferred the L or ES ones because he is convinced that the world is led by writers ("gens de lettres") (Interview March 2018).

The school put an emphasis on academic instruction as well as respecting cultural and religious diversity, and the environment in the French Republic. A glossy brochure made in 2004 to showcase the school is titled as follows: "a middle school in harmony with the Republic's values" "un collège en harmonie avec les valeurs de la République," a recurring feature of the schools I have been able to visit. The imagery reinforces this through a collage of symbolic pictures: the Arc of Triumph and the French flag in the background, with students in the foreground looking through a microscope and raising their hand enthusiastically as if to answer a question asked by a teacher, with the colors of the French flag dominating the color palette. A couple of charts show the evolution of enrollment, from 11 sixth graders in 2001 to 80 in 2004, adding one grade per year. The brochure features several quotes taken from the local and national press praising the school's academic success, the absence of proselytism, discipline and politeness, and the mix of two cultures. The brochure points out that the majority of teachers also teach in the public system, which helps to guarantee that the curriculum taught is the same. Several pictures show students in classrooms, boys and girls together, veiled and unveiled girls, looking through a microscope and playing soccer in the school, and others outdoors planting and learning about trees. Other pictures feature visits by politicians (mayors and préfet). The back cover showcases drawings from students.

The school did not have a uniform but a dress code which insisted on modest clothing, and decent hairstyle for boys. The headscarf was not compulsory, and the face veil (niqab) was forbidden in the school. Group prayers were held for those who wanted to.

Budget

Until 2006, the school managed to balance its budget, thanks to donations, tuition, and also buying repurposed or used materials. Before Meskine's arrest, tuition was 1500 euros, families and himself used to be very involved in collecting donations to keep the books in the black. However after his arrest, he felt limited in his activities as an imam by fear of the RG (secret services), so tuition had to be increased to 3500 euros a year. Meskine said that he paid the best salaries of all private schools, which led the school to its bankruptcy (Interview March 2018).

Student Selection and Demographics

Students were selected based on their school records and motivations. If students were forced by their parents and did not want to attend, they were not admitted. Parents had to agree that their students would take all classes (sport was given to me as an example they might want to avoid).

Over the years, they have had a couple of non-Muslim students, including a Catholic one; one of them insisted to take the religion class. According to Meskine, students came from all over the Ile-de-France area. Indeed, in one news segment, a student and her father interviewed note that they drive two hours to bring her to school in the morning.[4] Meskine remembers two families moved to be closer to the school. The majority of students were 2nd or 3rd generation, most of them middle class, with a variety of professions represented, including small business owners, computer scientists, and teachers. The school did have scholarships for students whose parents could not afford the tuition (Interview March 2018).

Extra-Curricular Activities and Field Trips

Students had to participate in a "classe verte" or countryside school trip in Normandy one week per year, which was fully integrated in the curriculum and graded, each grade with its specific program (Interview March 2018). Varied extracurricular activities included a calligraphy club, which did a beautiful calligraphy at the bathroom entrance about the importance of not wasting water (Picture 4.1).

Success

One of Réussite's goals was to show that "academic failure is not a fate in Seine-Saint-Denis" "l'échec scolaire n'est pas une fatalité en Seine Saint-Denis" (website). This was all happening in a climate when the Seine-St-Denis' school failures were so notorious that the Minister of Education in 1998, Claude Allègre, declared that there should be a bac 93,[5] essentially an easier version of the national high school exam for that area only (Constant).

The junior high had impressive results for the Brevet with pass rates of 100%, 93%, 100%, 100%, and 100% in 2005, 2006, 2007, 2008, and 2009; this in a department where the average was around 30%. The high school classes opened in 2005, and the first high school class obtained 100% success in the high school exam (Bac) in 2008. According to Meskine, Réussite was successful because they added an extra half an hour each for Math and French, enforced discipline and a safe environment for students to study, and were open to society at large through field trips in the countryside and guest speakers (firemen, City of science). In addition, they had evening classes for those who needed extra help. They kept traditional grammar classes that the National Education had cancelled before eventually reinstating them (Interview March 2018). In 2007–2008, the total number of students was 129 (website), but the school lost two-thirds of its students in 2015.[6]

Arabic

All students studied Arabic according to their level, 4 hours a week as an LV1 or 3 hours a week when they had two LVI. Meskine was very proud that they have had some outstanding grades on the Bac in Arabic, with some students earning 18/20 and 20/20 grades, which are quite extraordinary for the French system.

Picture 4.1 Mural in La Réussite's bathroom, Aubervilliers, March 2018. The Arabic calligraphy means "water is life" (an allusion to several Qur'anic verses that state that God created every living creature from water) and the French text "Water is life, do not waste it"

Religion Classes

Meskine added classes in Islamic ethics after 9/11 "to protect [children] from radical movements" (quoted in Bowen 114). Based on Bowen's class observation in 2006 of a religion class, where he explains that the teacher "alternates sessions on ethics with sessions on how to worship correctly" (120), the lesson "underscores a universalistic Islam, one that is particularly well-suited to life in a religiously pluralistic society" (121). The religion classes were called just that: religious education, an optional but graded class one hour a week covering the basics of Islam. The majority of students did not attend that class because they were too advanced for it. The classes focused on the five pillars, behavior, morals, respect of others. In addition, each year, students would learn some hadiths and suras from the Qur'an according to some progression (Interview March 2018).

Contract

The first request for a contract with the state was made in 2004, only three years after the opening of the school, thanks to a clause that stipulates an exemption that cuts the five-year waiting time down to three years when there have been more than 300 new lodgings built in the area. That first request was rejected because of a confusion over whether the director of the school was an employee or not. Réussite hired a principal the next year to clarify the situation, and refiled the request (Interview March 2018).

The year 2005 was when riots erupted in the north of Clichy-sous-Bois that eventually spread throughout the country. As it happened, Meskine was the imam of the Clichy mosque in the southern part of the city where things were under control, and for that very reason, he was accused by then-president Sarkozy of being dangerous. In addition, according to Meskine, Sarkozy was resentful toward him because the parents of the boys whose death sparked the riots refused to meet with him. Meskine said that he was threatened by Sarkozy, so he was not so surprised when he was arrested (Interview March 2018). This was a highly charged time during which a state of emergency was declared; several controversial pronouncements made by Sarkozy highlighted some of the problems that continue to plague France to this day, including marginalization of youth of immigrant origins.

In any case, Réussite School submitted all paperwork and underwent an inspection in June 2006 as part of the application to have a contract with the state. The inspector who came to the school told Meskine that he would write the best report he had ever written in his career. On June 19, 2006, Meskine was arrested on charges of terrorism. Meskine sarcastically commented to me that he had met several times with Sarkozy, would the police really have let the president meet with someone suspected of terrorism? The timing of the arrest was highly disturbing for the school, since June is the month during which students take the high-stake high school exam. Five days into his arrest, they still had not found anything against Meskine, so they combed the school's budget with a specialized team, arrested 17 members of the association that governed the school, and played them against one another, telling them that Meskine had denounced them. Under the pressure, they all signed documents accusing Meskine (except Meskine's son who was also arrested). The presiding judge, Philippe Croix, who would later on be implicated in the Bettencourt case, was not acting in an impartial way. It took eight years for him to be declared innocent on May 22, 2014 (Interview March 2018). Meskine insisted that the results that Réussite obtained over the years at national exams demonstrated that children in the 93 can succeed with little means, but that instead of "getting a medal, one gets handcuffed" "au lieu d'être médaillé on se voit menoté" (Interview March 2018).

Meskine asked Jean-François Cordé (then préfet of Seine-Saint-Denis) whether he should withdraw from the school. The answer was no, so Meskine stayed on. Three préfets came to visit the school between 2002 and 2010, all three tried to intervene with the Rectorat, but without any success. Over the years, there were numerous visits from various politicians, from the town's mayors, prefets, and representatives, and officials from Jewish and Catholic organizations who supported the school. Meskine assesses that politicians were fine with the project (the new prefet Balland came to a Ramadan dinner, and Sarkozy sent a congratulatory note to the school). An article even mentioned that the mayor and representative at the National Assembly spoke up in favor of the school (Ben Rhouma). It was at the level of the Rectorat that things got stuck (Interview March 2008).

Every time the request for a contract was filed, something would get in the way. In 2006, the Inspection office informed Réussite that it had forwarded its request for a contract to the Rectorat, yet in another letter, the very same office (Inspection académique) informed Réussite that they did not receive their file and it should be resubmitted, so Réussite had to start from scratch. Meskine even said that he asked the city hall so many times for a copy of the declaration of opening that employees there started to laugh. The school never saw any report written by inspectors, the last inspection was done in 2014. In 2015, inspectors came even though they did not submit an application for a contract that year (Interview March 2018). Several TV channels came, including France 2, which did a news segment in which a representative from the Créteil Rectorat said that they lacked the financial means to grant new contracts.[7]

In the meantime, the school had severe budget problems (Interview March 2018). In 2008 already, debts accumulated and the school closed its 11th and 12th grade classes because they were the most expensive to operate. In 2009, the association had over 350,000 euros in debt and justice intervened. When I consulted the website for the first time in 2013, it had not been updated since 2011. In Fall 2008, only 76 students returned to the school, down from 120 the preceding year. Despite impressive results at national exams in 2008, the school waited for an answer from the state for 8 years, only to have its request denied in 2014.

Some of the explanations given for that treatment are the fact that Meskine was arrested in 2006, two weeks after the Academy gave a favorable report for a contract (Bowen 130). The real reasons for his arrest are up for debate: was it because of Meskine's refusal to cooperate with the Secret services? Details of the arrest and explanations for all the baseless accusations levied against Meskine, support from local politicians and other faiths' leaders, as well as pre-electoral fever and gains that could be made from making arrests against prominent Muslim leaders can be found in Bowen's study (129–131). Meskine told me that he was seen as dangerous by the State because he had some control and influence over his mosque while being independent of the State; this is corroborated by a quote from the préfet in the newspaper *Le monde* cited by Bowen (43).

Matthieu Bidan, a journalist, tried to get answers from the Ministry of Education. When he reached out to the Minister of Education's cabinet, he was referred to the Rectorat, who did not reply. Bidan tried to contact some of the inspectors that visited Réussite, but they referred him to the Rectorat.[8] In another article published in 2008, here is what someone from the Rectorat had to say: that the high school would not be eligible for a contract until 2013, and that the middle school was not yet registered. The Rectorat says that the files to request the authorization to open the middle school were incomplete during all these years, something that Meskine counters by saying that the documents were sent multiple times.[9]

When I spoke with someone from the Ministry of Education in 2018, I asked about the case. From the point of view of the ministry, the middle school opened without following the proper procedure. The rectorat it depends on (Créteil) had a "benevolent attitude" and tried to help the school regularize its situation; but because the paperwork was not filled out properly, it took until 2013 for it to be formally declared. The Ministry also stressed that Meskine's brush with the authorities did not help the case of the school. Also from the point of view of the administration, the high school opened only in 2008.

However, Meskine showed me four thick files of correspondence and documents between the school and various authorities, meticulously ordered, with receipts showing that documents from the school were sent through registered mail. The correspondence deals with several simultaneous issues (the opening of the middle school, the opening of the high school, the application for a contract, each being a separate procedure requiring its own paperwork) and with different offices (city hall, préfecture, rectorat, inspection académique). It shows a Kafkaesque back and forth of requests of materials, with documents resent many times. There were several issues going on simultaneously that complicate the situation: some of the paperwork concerns the middle school and other the high school, there was some confusion about whether to open the high school as an extension or as a new school (which the Rectorat insisted they do), and changes in the director of the school necessitated resubmitting the entire file. There are clear inconsistencies coming from the Rectorat that seem to indicate a great deal of negligence and incompetence at best. There are numerous letters from Réussite indicating that they are resubmitting documents that have already been sent (including one three times). In December 2004, Réussite requested its registration number to register its 9th graders for the national middle school exam (Brevet) and their first batch of students took the exam. A letter from the Rectorat dated 2009 states that the middle school has never been properly registered, and that therefore it was not considered open and cannot ask for a contract until it is declared. And yet, every year, Réussite received a generic request for information sent to all schools not under contract asking to update their information, plus its students sat for the national exam, which implies that the school is on the Rectorat's books. Moreover, the Rectorat faulted Réussite for not being in compliance with the middle school's paperwork and used this as a reason to deny its eligibility for a contract with the state, yet the school was inspected in June 2006 for a contract, why would the Rectorat send an inspector to a school that is supposedly not open?

In a video following the denial of the contract request, one student points out the injustice of not being under contract, while numbers on the screen highlight the discrepancy between the percentages of Catholic and Jewish schools that are subsidized by the state (90%) versus only 2 out of 58 Muslim schools. Meskine is also interviewed and states that the school has met all criteria (administrative, pedagogical, safety), therefore there is a deliberate will to not fund the school. Ghada Ayadi, a French teacher, notes that Muslim schools are discriminated against because of the fear of radicalization, and notes that the school is actually a way to combat this phenomenon by giving kids the tools to succeed in French society.[10]

Closing

Contrary to the experience of some other schools, Meskine was full of praise for the media that came to Réussite because they were very objective. The school was always very open and has let in journalists to film and interview students over the years; 9/11 happened right after the opening of Réussite, and when the TV channel Canal+ showed up at the school unannounced, parents were opposed to letting them come to the school. Meskine convinced parents that the image of Muslims was already so bad it could not get worse. According to him, this was the best TV report on the school, with the school and the mosque in Montreuil calling for peace (Interview March 2019).

The building has been bought by an entrepreneur who will renovate and rent it; in the meantime, the school board will engage in a two-year reflection period to think about the next step. They hope to reopen in 2019–2020. Meskine's attitude was mixed: at the same time, a deep disappointment and bitterness that the school he worked so hard for did not receive equal treatment under the law, while maintaining a sense that he had done his duty and some optimism for the future. This was the first Muslim middle school in France, established where the National

Education failed, but there are doubts that authorities want to see success in Seine-St-Denis because it is a symbolic and sensitive department (Interview March 2018). This is a sentiment I heard elsewhere while trying to visit other Muslim schools in Seine-St-Denis.

The Réussite School was never affiliated with a mosque, something Meskine regrets retrospectively because in his opinion any school that wants to survive should be affiliated with some sort of organization. He also wondered if he should have accepted instead of refusing foreign donations, including one that would have required separating boys and girls (Bidan). According to him, Sarkozy and the organizations he imposed on Muslims have eradicated the Islam of France because they have been filled by people from the top and the media and forgot about people from the bottom. There are two different visions at odd, one is to build Islam in France with foreign governments, versus his vision of building Islam in France with the youth. According to Meskine, the former unfortunately prevailed. In 1999, he told a politician (Godard who was sent by Chevènement) that this approach was a huge mistake and predicted that it would lead to attacks 15 years down the road. Meskine estimated that it will take two to three generations to repair the damage that has been done.

Part II: IFSQY/Samarcande

I first heard about Samarcande in 2016 when I visited Eva-de-Vitray, one of whose founders mentioned it to me. I had not intended to visit it, as I selected schools that were pioneers and/or had a unique trajectory, but ended up including it for two reasons: first, having been referred by another school greatly facilitated getting approval to visit, and second, as it turned out, the reason that was stated for denying their first request for a contract is telling of current and future challenges faced by Muslim schools. Prior to my visit, I perused their website. I spent one day observing Arabic and religion classes in March 2018, speaking with teachers, and interviewed the principal and one of the founding members.

IFSQY (Institut de Formation de Saint-Quentin-en-Yvelines), also known as Samarcande school, clearly identifies itself first on its website as a Muslim middle and high school,[11] but has grown into a K-12 school. Samarcande is located in Montigny-le-Bretonneux, but to reach it through public transportation, I had to take the train to Trappes, a suburb that has made headlines in recent years for riots following a burqa check gone wrong in 2013.[12] Trappes has been labeled a "stronghold of jihadism in France" "un des bastions du djihadisme en France" following the high number of departures of its youth to Syria (quoted in Guéguen). Samarcande is located right at the edge of Trappes.

History

The middle school opened in 2009, the elementary and high schools were added in 2014 to answer parents' demands. As of 2018, they were not sure whether they would keep the high school or not. Samarcande's three educational objectives are listed in order: to achieve academic excellence, foster citizenship, and transmit a general knowledge of Islam. For the latter, it also mentions the ethical values that are common to monotheistic religions such as engagement, fraternity, and probity (website).[13] The website does not give any detail about religious education, but simply stresses its specificity as a Muslim school that accompanies students who wish to be guided in their spiritual awakening, knowledge of their religion, and carrying out the rituals.[14]

The principal has been involved with the project ever since it started in 2008; he has been the interim director of the school for the past five years. When asked about the main motivations for getting involved in this project, his reasons echoed those voiced by other schools: the local community in difficulty, with a lack of social mixing, low academic achievement, and problems in schools, particularly at the middle school level. Middle school is for many the place where the social divide (fracture sociale) starts, because students enter as children and leave as teenagers, the most difficult period when academic failures happen. So, instead of registering children in Catholic schools or prestigious public ones, this project was born out of a collective effort of concerned parents. He himself was raised and schooled in Trappes, but the schools have changed since then. The opening of another high school has exacerbated social segregation. Samarcande was established according to educational themes, not religious ones. The religious aspect of the school is to allow the expression and practice of religion. He considers Samarcande as a part of the National Education (Interview March 2018).

Mission, Curriculum, and Religious Character

The middle school's motto is exactingness and benevolence ("exigence et bienveillance"). Samarcande opened in 2009 with 6th and 7th grade classes totaling 32 students; the middle school now enrolls about a hundred students from 6th to 9th grade. The curriculum follows the national one. In addition, the middle school implements small-group learning, a personalized monitoring in basic subjects, and remedial work during breaks when needed to ensure students' success. Moreover, the school acknowledges the difficulties that can come with teenagehood and includes projects, workshops, and invited speakers on health, safety, addictions, solidarity, and academic advising among other topics to foster personal expression and self-fulfillment. As a measure of its success, the website mentions that 96 and 93% of the last two classes respectively obtained the brevet (the middle school graduation exam), including 50 and 79% with honors (cum laude/summa cum laude).

The subtitle states that the goal of the high school is to prepare students for selective higher education ("études supérieures ambitieuses"). The first paragraph starts by summarizing a study published by the Ministry of National Education that highlights the very high failure rate of students after their first year of college.[15] Given the high percentage of success at the bac (80%), selection has been moved to the first year of higher education. Therefore, the high school's role is not only to prepare for the national exam, the baccalauréat, but to prepare for success in college, and more specifically, for the most selective post-secondary education that each individual student can achieve. In order to attain that goal, the school demands high-quality work, emphasizes self-reliance and broad general education with critical thinking.

The website states that as the school is developing, it plans to first open a scientific section only, because it is the most popular nationally, and the one that obtains the best results at the high school exam (bac) and during the first year of university. Generally, this is the most prestigious track and the one that opens the most doors for higher education. While they do mention the possibility later to open other sections depending on demand, the registration forms for the 2018–2019 school year indicate that, at this point, they only have one 10th grade, and scientific 11th and 12th grades (http://ifsqy.fr). In fact, during our meeting, the director mentioned they were uncertain that they would keep the high school.

Contract and Budget

In 2014, the school budget of around 350,000 € was financed by parents (80%) and by donations (20%, Magassa-Konaté). The director cited the high school fee of 3500 euros as an obstacle, and he estimated that it would be lowered by half with a contract. There is only one class per level because of space limitations. In 2014, the school was stunned to have its first request to go under contract denied. In an article, the principal of the school expressed his shock at the unexpected news, given that an inspection of the middle school in January resulted in a favorable report. In February, a commission of the Rectorat also gave a positive recommendation for the request "pending availability of funds" (quoted by Magassa-Konaté). Despite clearing these steps, the rector of Versailles denied the request on April 2 in a letter citing "lack of funds"[16] (quoted by Magassa-Konaté). IFSQY was at the time the only Muslim school in what is the largest academy in the country (Le Bars); its 100 students were nothing compared to the more than 133,600 students in private schools under contract in that academy (Magassa-Konaté). The principal calculated that Samarcande's request would account for a mere 0.07% of the total. The article points out the fact that a Catholic high school that opened the same year as Samarcande was immediately granted a contract with the state (Magassa-Konaté). In another article, the principal debunked the financial argument by pointing out that the Rectorat had an additional 146 FTE to allocate, and that Samarcande's request totaled 8 FTE, which represented about 5% of the total additional means that were allocated for that year compared to the previous one (Le Bars). This could be an example of a disconnect between national and local authorities, with, on the one hand, recognition at the national level that Islam is behind in terms of infrastructure and that the state should help catching up, but, on the other hand, local officials and authorities not giving Muslim projects priority.

Samarcande lobbied local elected officials, and wrote to the préfet to alert them of the situation. They reapplied the following year and their request was granted. In a regional news segment taped right after the school had gotten a contract in August 2015 for its 6th grade class, the journalist said that there were 200 students from K-10.[17] A call for donations was posted on the website in 2015 to help repay an accumulated debt of 80,000 euros. In 2016, they applied for a contract for the 7th grade, which was only granted in 2017 (Interview March 2018). This shows that meeting all the required conditions and not having the kind of issues that a school like Réussite had is still not sufficient to be guaranteed a contract, and that Catholic schools have an edge, thanks to their wide network and organization. Unfortunately, such cases only reinforce the perception noted by Fredette that the lack of state assistance for the schools of the newest religion is discriminatory (94).

Student Selection and Demographics

Samarcande currently enrolls 100 students in the primary and 140 in the middle and high schools. There is an equal number of entering girls and boys, but more girls stay than boys, to a ratio of about 60:40. All socioeconomic backgrounds are represented. All families have a link with Muslim culture, be they Muslim (mostly from North Africa but also Turkey, Africa, Syria), converts, or mixed families (Interview March 2018). Motivations from parents are, first and foremost, academic achievement. As one teacher pointed out, if wearing the headscarf was the main reason, there wouldn't be any boys in the school. Two additional motivations are linked: parents want to protect their children from violence and failing peers that are commonplace in some public schools.

Applications are first done based on an evaluation of the academic file, taking into consideration grades, behavior, the interest of the family and child, and their support for the school's educational project. To that effect, the application file includes a section in which parents write a paragraph to explain their motivations to register their children in this school. For the middle school application file, there is an additional section similar to the parents' for students to fill to explain their motivation for being in the school (http://ifsqy.fr). Second, there is an interview with the parents to be sure that they subscribe to the school's project.

The school decided to prohibit the headscarf in elementary school for the next academic year. Their rationale: it is not an obligation at this age, and they want to allow for the development of the child. They do not admit handicapped children because they don't have the staff needed to do so. In a news report, a journalist pointed out that one-third of students drive 40 km to come to Samarcande, and that IFSQY has a waiting list and can only take half of the applicants. It is very rare that they make a student leave, but it has happened that they just couldn't handle/help a child (Interview March 2018). Class sizes showed 26 students for 6th and 7th grade, 21 for 8th grade, and only 14 for 9th grade.

Extra-Curricular Activities and Field Trips

The school does not maintain an updated online presence. The section of the website for the elementary school is under construction; it only states "the acquisition of solid basics" (http://ifsqy.fr/). The primary and secondary schools are separated by occupying different floors of the building. The Facebook page is not linked to the school's website, it is sparse with about five pictures of students in classrooms and announcements of a fundraising dinner, open house announcements, and a parenting workshop.[18] There are no traces of extracurricular activities as with some of the other schools that showcase them. During my visit, I learned by chance that students in the 10th grade requested philosophy classes, but since these classes are not offered until the 12th grade, the school will put together a workshop for them.

Arabic

Class schedules in the teachers' room showed that middle school students get two hours of Arabic a week, along with three to four hours of English and two hours of Spanish. The schedule for the 10th grade class only showed English and Spanish for foreign languages. Both Arabic teachers were graduates from the Sorbonne.

They do get students who have solid bases (for instance, one student used to attend the Algerian school in Paris and another one the Iraqi school), but these are exceptions. In the course of one of the conversations in the 6th grade class, a student exclaimed that in his family it was his great-grandmother who spoke Arabic.

Religion

According to the principal, what is particularly important for Samarcande is to give children the tools to succeed in a society where Islamophobia is rampant. They believe that all children have the ability to learn, and find it most rewarding when former students come to thank them. The school does organize a prayer during the break, and children whose parents have given their agreement are invited to pray.

According to the principal, the teacher for Muslim education was the last teacher to be hired, because it was not easy to find someone with a Bachelor's degree in Islamic sciences and a good knowledge of French society who can adapt the religious texts to the context of lived reality for students. They were looking for a different approach to teaching religion, one that applies knowledge to the current context, and that will help youth of Muslim culture to flourish in their country, that is, France in the twenty-first century. They want students to apply the values that are taught, starting with small projects. This was the one question that stumped most candidates whom they interviewed for the position: how to put values into practice? In addition, they want to avoid the dichotomy between haram/halal, and put an emphasis on quality over quantity. According to him, the worst risk would be to let religious people take over teaching, it has to be left to pedagogues (Interview March 2018).

Mrs. Ould Saïd is the person responsible for religion classes (or "éducation musulmane" "Muslim education" as she is identified on her mailbox in the teachers' lounge). She has a Master's degree in Islamic Sciences from the Institut Européen des Sciences Humaines, a private university affiliated with the UOIF that specializes in Islamic and Qur'anic sciences, and Arabic language. She has been teaching at Samarcande for 5 years and has designed the program with a clear pedagogical progression. Religion classes are called "éveil spirituel" or "Spiritual Awakening" in the elementary grades (3 hours a week); the classes are more like workshops. Only about half of students attend religion classes in the elementary school. In middle and high school, classes are called "Muslim religion" and last from 2 hours/week in 6th grade, down to one hour and a half in 8th and one hour in 9th grade; 85–90% of students attend the religion classes in middle school. There are currently no religion classes in the high school grades because they do not have a qualified teacher to teach. Some of the reasons given why some students would not attend the religion classes are as follows: some might want to privilege subjects such as Math, some take classes outside of school in their mosque, and others do not think Islam the same way as the teacher does. Based on discussions that ensued, I took that as a euphemism to say that some families might have a more traditional view of what religious education should be like; 85% of the curriculum is based on ethical values referenced in religious texts that aim to be relevant to students' lived reality. The program also includes famous people or organizations, including non-Muslim ones such as Mother Theresa, Nelson Mandela, and non-profits such as the Restos du Coeur.

Ould Saïd's teaching method fosters critical thinking. A lesson might be based on a text, for instance, a hadith on truth and lies, she will ask students questions to push them to think and explain what the text says. A majority of teachings emphasizes the notion of a social contract and the importance of human values, only about 10% of her classes are dedicated to the worship aspect, and always emphasizing how the spiritual dimension must have an effect on society. While there are written assignments that are evaluated, but not graded, she believes that the best proof of assimilation of knowledge is through good behavior. She prefers to help students understand the Qur'an over making them memorize it. When the news brings Islam-related topics, students usually want to talk about it and she will follow their questions. She likes to organize the program around themes, such as justice and injustice currently with the 9th grade class (Pictures 4.2 and 4.3).

Picture 4.2 Students collages ("who is this?"), Samarcande, Montigny-le-Bretonneux, March 2018, to illustrate the hadith: "The Prophet has said: There is no difference between an Arab and a non-Arab. There is no difference either between a white person and a black person"

Picture 4.3 A student poster, Samarcande, the French text states "to love one another is to believe, and to believe is to greet." This is an allusion to the following hadith: "You will not enter Paradise until you believe, and you will not truly believe until you really love one another. Would you like me to tell you something that would allow you to sincerely love one another? Promote greetings amongst yourselves"

Projects done by students decorate the walls of the hallways and show the wide range of topics and pedagogical approaches to the teaching of Islam. There are posters about the importance of greetings as a form of politeness and of exchange that is mentioned in a hadith by the Prophet: one student illustrated the hadith by writing hello in several languages next to the flag of a country where they are spoken. Another series of posters illustrate another Prophetic hadith about equality of all races and ethnicity[19] by having pictures of famous people changed beyond recognition by slicing them and mixing them up. Linked to that project were posters with quotes from famous people including Lamartine, St Exupéry, and MLK, on equality and racism. Another poster linked to a hadith about taking care of the earth illustrates a project about recycling, showing the content of a garbage can and how various items could be recycled. A letter from a well-known charitable organization providing free meals (Restos du cœur) thanks the school for their donations. That campaign was linked to the numerous injunctions in the Qur'an to feed the poor.

An example of one of many lesson plans she developed is about the status of animals in Islam. She was one of few religion teachers who could show me detailed lesson plans with clear objectives and applications (this does not mean that other religion teachers did not have that). The lesson, which aims to teach about compassion toward animals (and by extension preserve the environment), references the Qur'an (VI:38) and hadith, has clearly defined objectives (among them to preserve animals) and an application (build a bird feeder).

Notes

1. For an overview of the history of Seine-Saint-Denis and the failed government policies that have led to its contemporary problems, see Yamina Benguigui's documentary *93*.
2. https://www.youtube.com/watch?v=NLTW_O4bmMw.
3. https://www.youtube.com/channel/UCTge_ZLiTJ_mclvbIoB_CxA.
4. That segment which I watched on the web in 2013 has since been taken down for copyrights infringement. https://www.al-kanz.org/2009/11/02/reussite-aubervilliers/. It is now available at https://www.ina.fr/video/4032628001022.
5. 93 is the number for Seine-St-Denis' department (used for various administrative purposes, including zip code), and it is often referred to by its number.
6. https://www.youtube.com/channel/UCTge_ZLiTJ_mclvbIoB_CxA.
7. See https://www.ina.fr/video/4032628001022. Laurent Petrynka, identified as cabinet director at the Rectorat of Créteil, is interviewed and says in a snippet that the Rectorat does not necessarily have the means to fund new classes under contract.
8. « Cette question, j'ai voulu la poser au cabinet de Najat Vallaud-Belkacem. La communication de la ministre de l'Éducation nationale m'a gentiment renvoyé vers le rectorat chargé du dossier. Mais à l'académie de Créteil, pas plus de succès. Alors j'ai tenté de contacter directement deux des inspecteurs d'académie qui se sont rendus au collège, encore en janvier dernier. Ils m'ont tous les deux donné la même réponse: passer par le cabinet du rectorat. La boucle est bouclée… »
9. « Mais voilà, pour le rectorat de Créteil, le lycée ne pourra passer sous contrat que dans cinq ans à compter de la rentrée 2008, quant au collège,

« la période probatoire de cinq ans ne court pas encore », confie Laurent Pétrynka, le directeur de cabinet du recteur. Selon lui, les dossiers de demande d'agrément du collège et du lycée sont restés incomplets durant toutes ces années, retardant d'autant la période probatoire. « Faux ! » rétorque Dhaou Meskine, qui assure avoir adressé les documents requis à maintes reprises. » http://www.leparisien.fr/seine-saint-denis-93/le-college-musulman-en-faillite-veut-saisir-la-justice-18-09-2008-233858.php.
10. https://www.youtube.com/channel/UCTge_ZLiTJ_mclvbIoB_CxA.
11. http://www.ifsqy.org/. Consulted on 9 March 2018.
12. See "Trouble in Trappes."
13. « Transmettre les connaissances générales de l'Islam et faire vivre les valeurs éthiques qui transcendent les religions monothéistes telles que probité, engagement, fraternité, sens de l'effort, patience, partage… »
14. « L'établissement s'appuie sur son caractère propre musulman pour accompagner ses élèves qui le souhaitent dans leur éveil spirituel, la connaissance de leur religion et l'accomplissement de leurs rites. »
15. Samarcande's website mentions a study published in July by the Ministry of Education that states that less than 4 out of 10 students registered in the first year will move on to the second year of college. About 3 out of the ten students repeat the first year, and the remaining three abandon their college studies.
16. « En raison du manque de moyens, je ne peux donner de suites favorables à votre demande. »
17. https://www.youtube.com/watch?v=QDURYL6Juwc.
18. https://www.facebook.com/ecole.ifsqy?lst=100001420090921%3A100011958308349%3A1520614166.
19. « Le prophète a dit : il n'y a aucune différence entre un arabe et un non-arabe. Il n'y a pas de différence non plus entre un blanc et un noir » [« The Prophet has said: there is no difference between an Arab and a non-Arab. There is no difference either between a white person and a black person »].

References

Ben Rhouma, Hanan. « Aubervilliers: Réussite, une école musulmane en faillite. » *SaphirNews.com*, 13 Décembre 2008. https://www.saphirnews.com/Aubervilliers-Reussite-une-ecole-musulmane-en-faillite_a9575.html.

Bidan, Matthieu. « Le chemin de croix des écoles musulmanes. » *Streetpress.com*, 16 March 2015. https://www.streetpress.com/sujet/1426246444-colleges-ecoles-musulmanes-france.

Bowen, John. *Can Islam Be French? Pluralism and Pragmatism in a Secularist State*. Princeton: Princeton University Press, 2010.

Constant, Caroline. « La nouvelle colère des enseignants de Seine-Saint-Denis. » *L'Humanité*, 15 January 1999. https://www.humanite.fr/node/199291.

Guéguen, Elodie. « Trappes: 60 à 80 jeunes partis en Syrie. » *FranceInter*, 29 avril 2016. https://www.franceinter.fr/emissions/l-enquete/l-enquete-29-avril-2016.

Le Bars, Stéphanie. « Un collège musulman «sous le choc» après le refus de l'Etat de le prendre sous contrat. » *Le Monde*, 13 June 2014. http://www.lemonde.fr/education/article/2014/06/13/un-college-musulman-sous-le-choc-apres-le-refus-de-l-etat-de-le-prendre-sous-contrat_4437748_1473685.html#gDvHXeQud76Q1dc2.99.

Magassa-Konaté, Maria. « L'équité réclamée pour un collège musulman des Yvelines. » *SaphirNews*, 15 Mai 2014. https://www.saphirnews.com/L-equite-reclamee-pour-un-college-musulman-des-Yvelines_a18870.html.

No author. « Le collège musulman en faillite veut saisir la justice. » *Le Parisien*, 18 September 2008. http://www.leparisien.fr/seine-saint-denis-93/le-college-musulman-en-faillite-veut-saisir-la-justice-18-09-2008-233858.php.

No author. « Trouble in Trappes. *Violence erupts over the controversial burqa ban.* » The Economist, 27 July 2013. https://www.economist.com/europe/2013/07/27/trouble-in-trappes.

No author. « L'affaire Baby Loup en quatre questions. » *Le Monde*, 27 November 2013. https://www.lemonde.fr/societe/article/2013/11/27/l-affaire-baby-loup-en-quatre-questions_3520954_3224.html.

Peltier, Elian. "In France, Officer Slain After Swapping Places with Hostage Is Hailed as Hero." *NY Times*, 24 March 2018. https://www.nytimes.com/2018/03/24/world/europe/france-police-officer-arnaud-beltrame.html.

CHAPTER 5

Islamic Schools Future: Elementary Education (La Plume, Eva de Vitray) and New Trends (MHS, Salafi, Clandestine, Non-contracted Schools by Choice, and Homeschooling)

Elementary Education

The increase in trend to open elementary schools was already apparent in 2013 when I started this project. According to a recent report, it is part of a wider trend in private education in France. Data compiled by the Ministry of Education show that non-contracted schools remain a marginal phenomenon (0.5% of all students and 3% of the private, Billon 9), and Muslim schools represent less than 9% of schools not under contract (Billon 10). There has been a sharp increase in the number of schools and students enrolled in elementary schools that are not under contract, with 60% growth in the number of schools between 2010 and 2017, and 68% for the number of students in primary schools between 2012 and 2017 (Billon 12). Enrollment in Muslim schools increased by 28% in 2017, including 36% in primary schools (Billon 13).

La Plume

History
Established in 2001, La Plume was the first preschool and primary Muslim school. It is a precursor of the current trend even though it was established in a different social climate. The main impetus for the school started when a child came home using foul language after three

© The Author(s) 2019
C. Bourget, *Islamic Schools in France*,
https://doi.org/10.1007/978-3-030-03834-2_5

days in his public preschool. A group of friends, including the family of this child, joined forces to offer an alternative. So, before religion and Arabic, it was first and foremost the desire to provide an environment that would foster and transmit values of respect and politeness, which to the current director are still a priority over learning the Qur'an for instance. The director insisted repeatedly that she did not mean to indict the public system and underlined that the problems that plague the public school system are a reflection of society as a whole, characterized with a political system that is not in touch with educational needs, and where values have been lost because of social degradation. The school project was not a reaction to the social climate like it is today, it was born out of a concern for children. Not all the founders had children in the school. It opened with six students, added one grade per year until it reached fifth grade in 2007. Its enrollment reached over 100 in 2015 (Interview 2016).

The school is located in the southern part of Grenoble. It used to be housed in a building that belonged to the mosque next to it, but there was a desire to move away from the mosque. I met with the director of the school in September 2016, and spent the next day in the school, observing classes and interacting with the teachers. The school year had just started on the 15th of September, more than a week late according to French norms because they had just moved into a new building. They were renting the building, and were still not fully done adapting it to their needs (the parking lot was waiting for a fence to become the playground).

Mission, Curriculum, and Religious Character
The website[1] emphasizes the importance of education for the future generation of Muslims in France. The school's goal is to foster children's self-fulfillment through education of the whole person. La Plume stresses as its priorities the following: quality education as defined by the national curriculum, spiritual awakening, and learning Arabic. The logo of the school featured on the website mixes tradition and technology in a clever way, with the word plume written by an ink pen and the letter A written as an @. They do not have group prayers in the school because of the young age of students. They do not have veiled students, but occasionally some girls come back to school after the Friday prayer with a scarf on their head.

Contract and Budget

Their application for a contract with the State was denied in 2014 because of the inadequacy of the building that housed the school at the time (there was no outside space for a playground). They have also reduced the number of Arabic and religion classes, and will apply again now that they are in a better facility.

The school relies solely on tuition and donations for its budget; they hope to get a contract to lighten the families' contributions. They are not able to offer scholarships to underprivileged families. The move has led to many changes, and the director is handling all aspects. Contrary to other schools which have a broad support structure, La Plume is a two-women show, and the school depends on a huge personal investment on the part of the director and her assistant director. The director stressed that the financial situation of the school is always precarious. Fees were increased for 2016–2017 and were 175 euros a month. There are no plans to expand into a middle school.

Student Selection and Demographics

When I visited in 2016, the school had about 80 students, half of what it had the year before in part because they had to raise tuition by about 30 euros a month and because of the opening of a new elementary Muslim school in the same town.[2] They have roughly the same number of girls and boys, and all socioeconomic levels are represented in the school, but the increase in tuition does operate a selection, even though a few families that have stayed despite the increase must make sacrifices and tighten their belts to do so. One non-Muslim family was interested in registering their child because of the quality of the school, but did not because as a working family, they needed after-school activities that the school does not offer. Many families are of immigrant background, many from Morocco, one from Cameroon, but also a couple of Franco-French families.

Four years prior, they had a waiting list, some years over 400 students were waitlisted. In order to be admitted, families are interviewed to make sure that parents subscribe to the educational and pedagogical project of the school. Recently, two families were denied admission, not for lack of space, but because they had very conservative views about music.

Teachers
For the elementary level, teachers have a Bachelor degree, for the preschool a high school degree. The school trains its teachers to its own pedagogy following the Steiner method, which has gained great popularity in France as a whole, with many private schools following this pedagogy opening in recent years. As explained by the director, it consists in focusing more on the child than on the curriculum, following the child's questions, and using a lot of manipulatives for instance. Classes are limited to 15 students. She recalled a child that came to La Plume, who had a special assistant in the public school system and still could not read in fourth grade but who flourished there and learned to read in two years. Despite the fact that it was only their fourth day of classes when I visited, children seemed pretty well-adjusted already to their routine and new teachers.

Throughout its history, the school has depended on the personal investment of its staff. Up to a couple of years prior to my visit, the position of head of school had always been held by a man. Now the entire staff is working half-time. The staff has always been a female staff, because no man will work for the hourly minimum-wage salary (no paid vacation) that the school can afford to pay its teachers. All teachers are Muslim but the school regularly brings in non-Muslim guest speakers.

Extra-Curricular Activities and Field Trips
On their website and Facebook page, the school seems to be bustling with educational, creative, and fun activities. There are many pictures featuring, among other things:

- field trips to Chamonix building a snowman and luge, at the zoo, to a museum, a farm,
- artworks of all kind by students,
- incubating eggs and raising chicks,
- guest speakers (one with a beehive, one building elaborate structures with wood pieces).

Arabic
In preschool, children get two hours of Arabic per day. They plan on following the national programs for Arabic language teaching that were scheduled to be revamped that year for elementary school. The majority of children in the school do not have Arabic at home. By the end of preschool, they speak a little, by the end of elementary grades, they

have the grammatical basics, can talk about their daily routine, conjugate verbs in the present and past, and write a few sentences. English is added in Kindergarten.

Religion
The school's website stresses first and foremost the goal of fostering a respectful relationship between the child and the scriptures, based on a real understanding according to the child's intellectual capacities, so that they develop into a "blooming and enlightened Muslim citizen" "citoyen musulman épanoui et éclairé." The site also stresses what it is not, alluding to stereotypes of what a madrassa looks like: the school rejects "thoughtless and strict learning" but fosters progression through moderation. The director is very conscious of the difficulties faced by schools, who need to counter the erroneous perception that they are similar to madrassas. The director's motto is as follows: "il faut s'intégrer sans se désintégrer" "one must integrate without disintegration."

Under the heading "Discovering Islam," a list of questions shows the school's concerns over the difficult situation that their children are in, as religious families in a secular society where individualism and consumerism rule, at a time when Islam is constantly portrayed in a negative light. One question wonders "how to avoid having children torn in between two cultures?" Given this situation, the school's goal is to develop children's critical thinking and spirituality while providing a solid foundation on Islam.

The director insisted that the special character of the school consists in integrating values that are inherent in Islam in their pedagogy, such as generosity, sharing, empathy, respect, solidarity, etc. The school's goal is a transmission of values rather than a religious education. The school celebrates holidays and children make cards for Eid, for instance. The religion class is called "éveil à la foi" "faith awakening," it is optional but all students take it. It takes two forms: learning the Qur'an and a historical approach following the calendar of holidays and historical events. This class lasts a total of 1 hour a day over 4 days, and is spread out between the morning and a brief review in the afternoon. Children learn one *hizb* (1/60th of the Qur'an) over their three preschool years, and one *hizb* per year in elementary grades. The director had a disagreement with an inspector from the Academy about children learning the Qur'an; this was strongly criticized by the inspector who saw no purpose for it. The director argued that learning the Qur'an is equivalent to the memorization of poetry that is part of the national curriculum, but the inspector refused to consider it as equivalent (Picture 5.1).

Picture 5.1 Eva de Vitray, Mantes-la-Jolie, September 2016

Eva-de-Vitray

History

The "founding fathers" of Eva de Vitray are eight childhood friends, whose parents founded the first mosque in Mantes-la-Jolie. They do credit the fact that their parents, some of them illiterate, have given them a model of what grass roots action can accomplish for a community. Their project was in great part prompted by violence in public schools and beyond. They see education as the key, and rather than engaging in victim discourses, they decided to roll up their sleeves and create a school. They spent two years preparing for it, starting with debating the fundamental question as to whether there should be a Muslim school in their town. One of the founders, Youssef Aallam, who was my primary contact, initially refused to be part of it, because he is a staunch supporter of public education. As he pointed out to me, all the founders of the school are a product of the public school system, and he himself is a teacher in a public junior high school. All but one of the founders had children enrolled in the school in 2016, and they all paid full tuition. The founders I met (all but one) were very enthusiastic about the school and eager to share their vision. They are often solicited for advice by people who want to open schools. Most of the time they discourage them, because the vast majority of those who have sought their guidance do not have the expertise needed, a well-defined educational project, nor realize the amount of work needed to pull it off. They attribute their rapid growth and success to the fact that they have a similar background and knew each other well, draw on their different areas of expertise (in education, in business, in local politics), were willing to make financial and time sacrifices, and had the support of their family. Aallam distinguishes their project from others that were in reaction to the law against the scarf or other things. Eva de Vitray was conceived as an educational project from the very beginning, as a Muslim school with spiritual awakening and also as a way to counter a Salafist project. They decided to start with first grade[3] to accompany students from the start. The school is an expression of the National Education, not a competition.

Bilingualism came after, and they did argue about whether English or Arabic should take center stage, but not religion. One of the founders advocated to start with a middle school, but everybody else favored the elementary level so that children could be impregnated with Eva de Vitray's school spirit at a young age, and not at the beginning of teenagehood which is a difficult age. After they added middle school grades, students from another Muslim school who entered Eva de Vitray at the middle school level needed remedial action against using foul language.

One of the founders is a savvy local politician. Before opening the school, they spoke about their project to the mayor and to people from political parties from the left and the right, to pre-empt opposition. The week after my visit, they had invited a senator to come and visit the school. They emphasized this preliminary groundwork of communicating with local administrators and parties done before and during the elaboration of the project.

It took a while to find the name of the school: they wanted a woman's name, and not a name from the Arab-Muslim heritage, in order to translate their cultural rooting in France. Eva de Vitray-Meyerovitch, the first to translate Roumi's *Mathnawî* in its entirety in French, had a traditional Catholic upbringing, a Jewish husband, and converted to Islam after the reading of Iqbal's book *Recontruire la pensée religieuse de l'Islam* led to Roumi and Sufism and triggered her discovery and conversion to Islam when she was 40 years old. Her life is a symbol of the Abrahamic traditions that the school refers to when it situates its special character (Picture 5.2).

The school board has different people in charge of various areas: education, administration, technical/maintenance, development, finance. They are all volunteers except the one who directs the school full-time. This is a big time commitment as they meet once a week to discuss school issues. The Wednesday before my first visit, they had a meeting that lasted until 1 AM as they were putting the last touches to the application to get a contract with the state. After volunteering this information to me, the school principal added that their wives are involved in the project by taking care of the family while they stay out late for school business. He might have had in mind one of the comments left on the school's Facebook page about the absence of women on the school board.[4] The pedagogical aspect was the last thing they put in place, they worked in the beginning with Karima Mondon who is known for helping with alternative projects.[5]

Eva de Vitray is located in Mantes-la-Jolie, which Alec Hargreaves characterizes as a "provincial *banlieue*" because it is too far from the city (50 miles west of Paris) to be considered a suburb, yet it shares many

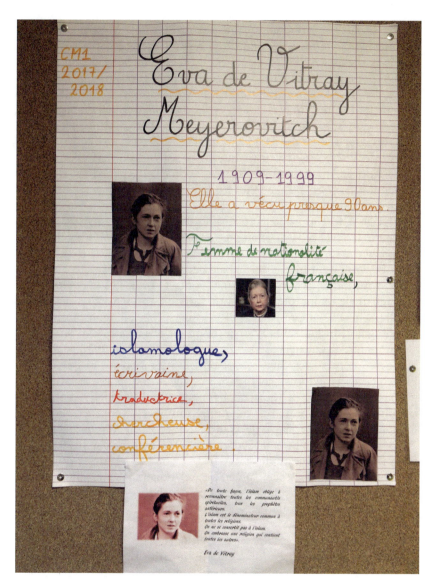

Picture 5.2 4th grade students' poster, Eva de Vitray. The quote by Eva de Vitray at the bottom translates as: "In any case, Islam forces one to recognize all spiritual communities, all prior prophets. Islam is the common denominator of all religions. One does not convert to Islam, one embraces a religion that contains all others"

of the social ills attributed to the *banlieues* (611). Mantes-la-Jolie has become synonymous with one of its housing projects, the Val-Fourré, which is the largest HLM estate in France, with "28,000 inhabitants. This represents three fifths of Mantes' total population, though the estate covers only one-fifth of the town's surface area" (Hargreaves 610–611). Eva de Vitray is in the Val Fourré quarter, whose population, according to information given in a podcast in 2015, is 80% Muslims and 36% foreign (Bastide and Dupiot).

Eva de Vitray was the first Muslim school and only Muslim elementary school in the department of the Yvelines. It opened for the 2012 academic year with 60 students from K-3rd grade, opening one additional grade per year, and has experienced a steady growth: 109 students in 2015 in K-5, 150 students in K-6th grade in 2015, 168 in 2016 when I visited. It reached 190 students from K-8th in 2017, and there are a projected 210 for the next school year. In 2016, I was told that the school payroll went from 5 to 32 paid employees in 4 years.

As with other schools, my first contact with Eva de Vitray was through their online presence, both through the school's website and Facebook page.[6] It presents itself as "une école bilingue musulmane" "a bilingual Muslim school." The home page includes a video clip of a five-minute segment shot by France 2 in October 2013 which was broadcast as part of a news report on private schooling in France. The French flag that adorns the entrance of the school is not "a strategical posture," states one of the school founders and president of the association. This was repeated to me during my visit by another one of the founders: The tricolor flag reflects their well-thought educational project.

I visited Eva de Vitray in September 2016 and in March 2018. The school, located within a short bus ride from the Mantes-la-Jolie train station, is housed in several prefabricated buildings (including one for the middle school and one for the primary school), a cafeteria, a library, offices, and two playground areas.

Mission, Curriculum, and Religious Character
The school follows the national curriculum with the addition of Arabic language instruction and an emphasis on Islamic values. The educational project is rooted in French national values in two ways: by stressing forming citizens in the value of the Republic and by presenting the creation of the school as an action grounded in citizenship. The Muslim character of the school is widened by situating it in the Abrahamic

tradition and focusing on spiritual humanism. In addition to stressing the value of citizenship and being informed to exercise one's rights and responsibilities as citizens, the educational project as presented emphasizes the diversity it brings to the educational offerings, its opening to society at large, and the importance of children's development, including spiritual.

Eva de Vitray will not go beyond 9th grade (the end of middle school in France), because they want students to go out in the wider community, and exchange with non-Muslims. They are very aware that their school is a cocoon of some sort, and view it as very important that once they reach high school, they get mixed in with the general population, because in the words of the principal, "it is an important time to exchange with the other." They see Eva de Vitray as a secular school because they respect each individual choice, discourage discourse of haram/halal and are happy that children have stopped using these terms.

Eva de Vitray does not have an official affiliation with the local mosque, and unlike many other schools did not start in a mosque, but collects donations every Friday and invites guest speakers in its classes. There is no prayer room for lack of space; children are free to pray but not in groups. School is in session on Friday afternoons. The school discourages girls from wearing a headscarf before they reach puberty because they want children to come to Islam out of conviction, and not out of imitation, and to be at peace with themselves. An unusual decision has been taken by the school: they offer meatless school lunches to break with halal issues that dominate in the media, and because one does not need meat to have a balanced diet.

Contract and Budget

From the beginning, the goal was to have a contract with the state, which will help lower school fees and bring a certain stability. When they first applied in 2016, they had a favorable report from the inspection, and in 2017, Eva de Vitray became the first elementary Muslim school on metropolitan soil to have a contract with the state, but the Academy invoked a lack of funds so only the first grade class was put under contract. They were inspected again in February 2018 and are hoping to have first and second grades under contract the following year.

In 2016, about 45% of the school budget was covered by tuition and fees, 40% by a Circle of Friends group composed of 50 businessmen, and the rest by donations. All families pay tuition and fees. The tuition and school fees posted on the registration documents for academic year 2016–2017 were 1900 euros/year for elementary school and 2200 for middle school (not including fees for materials/activities, building acquisition), for total dues of 2410 euros for elementary. For school year 2018–2019, fees remain the same for elementary classes not under contract, but is lowered to 1710 for classes under contract with participation of the local administration for materials/activities fees. Middle school fees now total 2710 euros, and none of these classes are under contract.

Student Selection and Demographics
According to the principal, in 2016, there were slightly more boys enrolled (93) than girls (86); 66% of students are children of professionals, and 99% are 2nd and 3rd generation. The school accepts all children but does conduct an interview with parents before admission to make sure that they subscribe to the educational project. If parents pass the interview, they sign a convention with the school. Some of the questions ask what parents think about the fact that students go to the swimming pool and play music. These types of questions are clearly meant to "weed out" very conservative families who would object to such activities. Demand for the school is high, every year they deny hundreds of applications for lack of space (they get up to seven applications per spot for some classes).

During my first visit in 2016, they had one non-Muslim student from a practicing Catholic family and hoped to welcome more in the future. It is interesting to note that there is a Catholic school nearby, but that this family chose Eva de Vitray instead. In a podcast recorded during an open house at the school in 2015, various parents interviewed cited the private aspect and the level of education as their first motivation to enroll their children, and religion as an added bonus (Bastide and Dupiot). In the same podcast, a nine-year-old girl complained about her former classmates who made fun of her in a Catholic school.

Teachers
All teachers have passed the national recruiting exam or have worked in the field of education, some have an MA1 in education. Only about one third of teachers are Muslim, the main criteria for hiring is qualification, respect for the educational project of the school, and vision of the benevolent role of the adult in the education of children. The school offers workshops to help teachers take the national competitive entrance exam.

During my first visit, it was mentioned that the school has hired some teachers and supported and coached them to get the qualifications they needed.

They had some difficulties with the only teacher who was under contract when they started the 2017 school year. She grew dissatisfied because she had to teach an extra 15 minutes every day compared to the public system and wanted to change the class schedule. She was terminated and everyone seemed very happy with the new teacher. I met the latter during lunch and she had yet to be paid after more than 2 months because she is paid directly by the Ministry. This transitional period of being partially under contract creates a two-tier system for teachers.

Extra-Curricular Activities and Field Trips
Among the pictures that were part of the slide show on the front page of the school website in 2016, we see children (boys and girls together) in a swimming lesson and during a field trip to a museum. On the Facebook page, one can see various activities, including a chess tournament, community service ("opération Berges saines" nature clean-up), literary guest speaker with a writer, a Veteran's Day ceremony at the city hall, and a theater project with a local association.

Arabic
Eva de Vitray labels itself as a bilingual school with the goal of making Arabic the language of instruction for some subjects. Arabic is offered 5 hours a week in elementary and 4 hours a week in middle school, and in small class sizes (classes are split into 2 groups according to their level). The manuals are chosen by the person in charge of pedagogy, and follow the CEFR. Starting in fourth and fifth grade, Arabic becomes a language of instruction. One example I was given was a multidisciplinary project for a vegetable garden in the school that draws on maths, Arabic, and religion. Arabic is not the only language, children also get 45 minutes a week of English instruction in elementary school.

Religion or Spiritual Awakening
This optional class is called "éveil spirituel" or spiritual awakening in the elementary grades. The description on the website stresses spiritual awakening, teaching ethics by example, and learning through experiencing the immediate environment, nature. Additional examples that were given to me during my first visit were to respect the environment, animals,

and to develop ethical values and critical thinking. The teacher can use a theme as a spring board (for instance, the environment), and then bring out religious references pertinent to it. It is scheduled in the morning for 20 minutes so that students who don't want to attend it can arrive at 8.30 when classes start, but they are attended by all students. There are three teachers (called "intervenantes" or speakers) every week who rotate among the classes, each with a specific focus: one teaches ethical behavior, the other Qur'anic recitation, and the third "nasheed" or religious songs. In a brief discussion I had with one of them, who is an elderly lady from Algeria who volunteers at the school, she explained that she likes to emphasize the kindness of the Prophet, and that we should treat our children in the same way. The goal is for students to learn while having fun, and the founders insisted that spiritual awakening takes place all day long every day.

In the middle school, they add a "Culture, Civilization and Ethics" component. In 2016, this class was taught by a former teacher of SES, who was a doctoral student in sociology. In a brief conversation, he explained to me that he was given carte blanche by the school to teach those classes. His approach is philosophical, and he wants to give students some foundation through philosophical exercises. He favors provoking questioning from students, so that the new generation will bring its own answers to questions that are asked by and for this new generation. That teacher has since left and classes are now taught by one of the founders. The school is in the process of creating a curriculum for the middle school grades to push students to develop critical thinking. The week prior to my visit, they spoke about the attacks. They were happy that children have stopped talking about hell and haram.

New Trends

A Secular School with Muslim Ethics: Lycée MHS

After seeing MHS on a list of Muslim schools on the web,[7] I took a quick glance and thought there might have been a mistake, because nowhere on MHS's website is there a specific reference to Islam. I noticed a high proportion of students wearing a headscarf, and the names of the founders and many teachers point to an Arabic heritage. After emailing the school, I received a response that confirmed that indeed, it was not a confessional school but a universal one that accepts all religious signs and practices but teaches none. Given the high number of Muslim students and outreach to Muslims, I included it in my study as one example on one end of the spectrum of schools that fulfill a need of the Muslim community.

History
According to the president of the school, MHS was founded as an answer to the crisis that plagues education and to the sociocultural divide. She had always wanted to start a school, and was involved when young with volunteering through city halls and cultural associations in after-school tutoring. What really triggered her into action was the low level of student performance she witnessed as a volunteer tutor. She herself went to a private Catholic middle school, for reasons having more to do with the strict discipline than with academics. At the time, the academic levels between the private and the public were very similar, but now she thinks there is a significant gap between the two.[8]

She was dealing with students who previously attended Muslim schools in a religious environment, and whose parents were putting emphasis on the religious and not on academic success. She saw these youth living in a cocoon, and was worried to see the new generation of her community sink into mediocrity because of an anti-system feeling and a discourse of victimization. The project was conceived to provide an academic and intellectual school, as well as improve the image of Muslims.

She contacted the other two founding members, one of whom she had met in a religion class, the other through her little sister whom she tutored. They met and realized that they were on the same wavelength, planned the school in three months, and opened in September 2015 in the Tour Montparnasse with 60 students. When asked about the fact that they are three women, the director answered that it was just by chance (Bey). The school board has a president (also the director of the school) with a background in management who has been active in associations for more than fifteen years, a vice-president with a background in economics in charge of commercial development, and a treasurer with a background in finance.

MHS first opened as a school under Muslim ethics. A Facebook post in July 2016 and a radio interview identify MHS as the first Muslim Ethics High School registered in the Academy of Paris. According to the director, it was unfortunate that more than 50% of parents were attracted by the religious label, and not the academic project. There were issues that were impossible to deal with, as an example, once a girl screamed when a boy touched her shoulder. Parents complained because they wanted Qur'anic and religion classes. As a result, many students were dismissed and they only had 20 enrolled the second year. In 2017, they moved to a new place. This is the only school with any connection to Islam located in Paris intra muros. It is a cramped facility on the first floor of a building. There were 44 students enrolled in the school when I visited in Spring 2018.

Mission, Curriculum, and Religious Character
MHS now labels itself as the first universalist high school in France. It offers the scientific (S) and socioeconomic (ES) tracks. It plans to add management and business administration (STMG) and ninth grade in Fall 2018, even though ninth grade is typically part of middle school, in order to make sure that students have solid basis to tackle the rigorous high school curriculum, as well as a BTS (a post-secondary degree). Class size is capped at 16 students. The high school is universalist in the philosophical and moral senses: it respects all people and promotes a universal code of ethics (http://meohighschool.org).

The three core precepts of the school are: respect of all individuals and their values, a student-centered educational approach, and a strict ban on proselytizing (http://meohighschool.org). The emphasis is on quality and personalized education, so as to give students confidence to become responsible citizens and to foster social cohesion. The school emphasizes critical thinking and autonomy, and values respect of all individual, solidarity, and individual freedom conditioned by knowing how to be in a diverse society ("le savoir être et le «vivre ensemble»"). The director is very strict on respect, school rules and life skills, because students can be insolents. She referred to an incident when she scolded a girl who was chewing gum (Interview 2018).

MHS stands for Méo High School, Méo being an acronym for «Méthode One Plus» which refers to the school's pedagogy that draws from Jean Houssaye's pedagogical triangle which consists in finding a balance among the relationships between student, knowledge, and teacher.[9] The «Méoplus» brand is trademarked by an Institute of the same name, presented as a center for adult training, which is registered in the names of the three founders of Méo High school.[10] A tutoring system is a core element of the high school project, because of the personal support it provides, be it remedial or to get ahead. It is set up and coordinated by a student from the ESSEC Business School, and draws on university students in various disciplines (science, literary studies, and languages).

The school rules, posted at the reception on the board, state that students should wear proper attire, and address some Muslim articles of clothing, with an explicit ban on jilbabs and niqabs (and also on pants with holes, caps, sunglasses, short dresses and skirts), but wearing a headscarf is explicitly authorized. Moreover, an entire page is devoted to explaining the benefits of PE classes and the rules pertaining to PE, which addresses two issues: the fact that the school uses a gym outside, and to stress that this is a compulsory class and cannot be missed without a valid reason. Students are free to pray if they wish.

The school's only religious character is the visible affiliation of many of their students to Islam. When asked why the school was not named after a famous Arab figure, the director answered that the school is neutral and wants to remain so, and not be linked to any philosopher, scientist, or else. She insisted that MHS is not a religious school but a school with a Muslim ethics, and that Muslim ethics is universal, and includes being open to others. They have a benevolent attitude toward personal development, therefore religious signs are accepted "within reasonable limits," hence the ban on the burqa and niqab (Bey). In my discussion with the director, she repeated that they are positioning themselves as focused on academic excellence, because the spiritual belongs to the personal domain. They do indirectly teach some ethics through universal values that are inculcated through other subjects. As an example, the setting up of a BDE or student association is a way to open to others while getting them involved in a project instead of taking a class. When I asked her why not add an optional religion/ethics class to satisfy parents' demands, she categorically said that if she had to add one class it would be an extra hour of math or French.

Contract and Budget
The school depends on donations for its budget; the two other founding members are in charge of that aspect. They are independent and want to remain so, and do not collect in mosques because they do not want to jeopardize their future application for a contract with the State. In a radio interview, the director said that they are looking into loans but regular banks do not correspond to their ethics and Muslim banks do not yet finance these kinds of projects (Bey).

Tuition is 4000 euros per year, and this leaves 5000 euros per student per year that must be covered by donations. They do a lot of fundraising that targets Muslims, such as a video wishing a merry Ramadan while calling for donations citing the following saying from the Prophet: "the best present from a father to a child is a good education."[11] Also the school had a booth at the annual meeting of the RAMF (the largest meeting for Muslims) in 2016.

Student Selection and Demographics
Of their students, 99% are Muslim, 1% of mixed background. More than 50% of their students came from other Muslim schools. In the beginning, they had about 90% of their students who were female, now it is about 50%, and 95% of the girls are veiled. This is the only school I visited where none of the female staff I saw wore hijab. Students come from middle-class families. Selection of students is done based on content and cognitive tests to assess their knowledge and help determine students' potential, and an interview with the parents and students (students also have to write a statement of purpose as part of the application to gauge their motivation). Two students at least came from far (Aubervilliers, a suburb on the other side of Paris).

Teachers
The director, who also teaches math, seemed to be the driving force behind the school, helped by the counselor (CPE), who was very enthusiastic and eager to speak about the school. While I was there, the director moved from the front desk (while the CPE was having lunch) to the classroom where she taught math, to the principal's office (where she received me and later on parents). All teachers are part-time with MHS, some by choice because they also teach in other schools. MHS is the only school that lists a small biography for its teachers and principal on its website. Some teachers have Master's and Ph.D. degrees.

Extra-Curricular Activities and Field Trips
There are pictures on the Facebook page of outings to places including the Drancy camp, the Louvre, and the tribunal (Palais de Justice). There is also a video taken during a career fair where students had the opportunity to meet professionals representing different career paths.

Success
The first class that MHS graduated had 83% success at the bac in 2016, and these were students who only attended MHS in their last year of high school; some of them had been home-schooled because they wear a headscarf and had great deficiencies to catch up (Bey).

Arabic
Arabic is offered as first, second, or third foreign language, two hours a week. They follow the national program. Twenty-nine out of the 44 students enrolled were taking Arabic in 2018. Other languages offered are English and Spanish.

Salafi, Clandestine, Non-contracted Schools by Choice, and Homeschooling

During my first visit in 2016, I was told by one member of Averroes that a documentary by reporter Bernard de La Villardière on Islam in France, which he anticipated was going to be slanted and tendentious, was about to air on national TV. "L'islam en France: la République en échec" "Islam in France: The Defeated Republic," broadcast on September 28, 2016 on channel M6, announces its bias in its very title. Though the documentary does include moderate Muslims, such as stand-up comedian Samia Orosemane and imam Abdelali Mamoun (who insists that one can be a secular and Republican Muslim), the overall report focuses more on controversies and extremism.

In addition to featuring Averroès,[12] it included a segment on APCS/Al-Dirayah, a school it labeled as Salafi, located in Sevran, in Seine-St-Denis, where the Salafi discourse and its ideology are wreaking havoc. In this town of 50,000 people, 15 youths left for Jihad in Syria (this is fifteen times higher than the national average). The mayor, Stéphane Gatignon (from the Green party) is accused of having let the Salafis gain hold of his town in exchange for votes.[13] One example is that he has authorized a private Muslim school (APCS association pour le savoir et la connaissance) on city land. When Villardière came to film the school, he was denied access by the director (who is known by another interviewee as someone who refuses to shake hands with women), but they could see that most of the girls on the playground were veiled. During an interview with Villardière, the mayor justifies his decision to encourage this project because these children were not in school, and having them in a school registered with the Ministry of Education is the only way to ensure some control.[14]

While looking for APCS school to include it in this study, I noticed an increase in the number of Muslim schools and projects in the Seine-St-Denis department, which is not surprising given that one-third of all residents in Seine-St-Denis are Muslims (Laurence and Vaïsse 7). Because of the notoriety of department 93, I felt it was particularly crucial to include what is happening in that area (in addition to La Réussite covered in Chapter 4) and reached out to several schools, in vain. I had to be persistent to various degrees to get a response from all schools (except one that answered immediately my very first email), this is not to say anything negative about any of the schools, who have more pressing things to do than answer a researcher's questions. Therefore, I decided to try my luck and just show up at some schools (and in the process of walking around even discovered one I had not heard of), but this did not yield any results. I include a brief summary below about the limited information I gathered in the process.

Salafi School? APCS/El Dirayah
If it is indeed Salafi as claimed in La Villardière's documentary (but denied by the director, see Brancato), APCS seems to contradict the 2010 report which states that the most extreme fringes such as the Salafis do not invest in this type of project for doctrinal reasons or because of the visibility it brings (Bras et al. 74). Although their website is listed in a compilation of Muslim schools,[15] it has been removed and no information is available other than a short blurb on a website cataloguing all Muslim schools in France. This might be in part due to the publicity brought about by the documentary. In any case, I had to go to the city hall to get the address. The person in charge of education said that according to their records, about thirty children are declared in that school. These records are probably out of date.[16]

When I showed up unannounced at the school, I first saw the pre-school playground. Children were playing outside, all little girls were bareheaded and dressed up with Disney-style princess dresses because of a Medieval theme festival they were having that day. I spoke with a teacher who came to the gate but she couldn't let me in because the director wasn't there. I learned that the elementary school has one section for each grade 1–5, with about twenty children in each class. I walked further around and saw another group of children playing on a basketball field, this must have been some of the elementary school children. I could spot three girls wearing a headscarf out of maybe ten or so. I left my contact information, and called to follow-up, but never heard back.

Clandestine School? Amana
While looking online for APCS, I found another school in Sevran: Amana.[17] Though they claim to provide after-school support only, it is widely assumed otherwise (including by the city hall). There are small indications here and there that cast doubts. Their website projects a very conservative image, with two different contact phone numbers (one for women and another one for men). There are pictures of field trips, and descriptions of core and religious curriculum.[18] After several unanswered phone calls to the number for women, I called the one for men and had a conversation explaining my project. I was told that this was not a full-time school but only after-school support, and that he would transmit my contact to APCS. I never heard back.

I went there anyway and happened to arrive as young children were let out around noon on a Wednesday, and was easily let in by one woman, and instructed to climb a flight of stairs to talk to someone responsible for the school. Once there, two women told me they couldn't answer my questions and would give my contact to the person in charge. Even though she refused to talk about the school, one of them did engage in a 20-minute conversation about school failure in Seine-St-Denis and the lack of government support to fix the public schools. There were posters on the walls in the staircase, one showing children's names next to their art, an Andy Warhol inspired drawing of hands. While Amana might be a full-time school disguised as an after-school program, other schools are completely hidden, such as the one uncovered in this news segment, also in Seine-St-Denis.[19]

Non-contracted by Choice? Fort School
One should distinguish between schools that are not under contract but that do aim for one (the majority of Muslim schools), and those that do not. There is a small percentage of private schools in France who are past the five-year mark that allows them to request a contract with the state but that do not, in order to maintain control over their curriculum, be it for religious reasons, pedagogical approach, or level (one school wants to maintain standards higher than the national ones). Fort School presents

itself on its main page[20] as "hors contrat." I had several conversations over the phone with the principal trying to set up a visit, in the course of which he said he was not sure a contract was the way to go for the school, but I do not know the reliability of the information he gave me. After leading me on, the director eventually said I would not be able to visit the school, but agreed to an interview, to which he never showed up. I was unable to reach the owners directly.

Homeschooling and Distance Learning
According to a news report, there has been a 36% increase in homeschooling in the last three years.[21] There are a variety of options for homeschooling in France. One is to register students through the CNED (National Center for Distance Education), authorization must be granted by the Rectorat for tuition not to be charged. Home-schooled children can also be registered with private distance education companies and since 2007 an annual pedagogical inspection is required. Homeschooled children not registered through the public or private distance education programs must be registered with the city hall and the Rectorat, and must be inspected annually by the Rectorat for pedagogical control and every other year by a social worker from the city hall (Puzenat 234–235). These regulations for homeschooling children were confirmed by a parent: declaration with the city hall, and inspections by a social worker sent by the city hall to verify that schooling takes place in an adequate environment, and by an inspector from the Academy to verify that core academics are taught.

Some families who homeschool pool their resources together and take care of groups of children at one's home or in a mosque, while the children are registered as homeschooled and in distance classes (Puzenat 227–231). Several Muslim schools have actually started as after-school tutoring or support for students registered through distance learning, including Averroès and La Réussite as detailed earlier. In Seine-St-Denis, The Fort School association was founded in 2011, and for 2 years provided after-school tutoring, language classes, workshops, and field trips, leading to the opening of the elementary school in 2013. The middle and high school Fraternité on the first posting on their Facebook page shows the school recruiting for the newly opened 10th and 11th grade in March 2015, specifying that the middle school has been registered with the academy and a comment clarifying that students will no longer need to register with the CNED.

Another example is Al Andalus, which was the only functioning K-12 school that had a booth at the 35th RAMF on March 31, 2018, where I went in the hope of finding schools represented. The school is part of an association that opened in 2000 and that over the years added various offerings such as after-school tutoring, Arabic and Islamic classes for children and adults. It opened a school in 2012 whose goal was to accompany families who chose to homeschool, the following year they started working on the creation of a full-time school, which they were authorized to open in 2016. In the course of my discussion with one of the parent volunteers manning the booth, she explained to me that she used to homeschool her children before putting them in the school, for the same reasons I heard in other schools: academic achievement, safety, manners, Muslim environment. In the course of our conversation, I learned that Muslim families who homeschool feel particularly scrutinized during mandated inspection visits.

Conclusion

I can surmise that several reasons played a role in my difficulties to get access to these schools. First, many schools, especially in the beginning, struggle and their staff are so stretched that they cannot spare any time. This might be the main reason, and a very understandable one. Second, the constant negative coverage of Islam in the media has led to a lack of trust. Many people during my initial contacts with most schools assumed that I was a journalist and I had to explain I was not. Because the Seine-St-Denis department has particularly suffered from such coverage, the mistrust might be higher there. This is evident in the reactions to La Villardière's documentary. Third, some of these schools are extremely conservative, as indicated by the two different contact phone numbers for men and women. While the cowl does not make the monk, and I only got a glimpse, one school was overall the most conservatively dressed crowd of teachers/parents I saw. One student I met at MHS had gone to one of these schools for one year and complained that it was much too strict and gave me the dress code as an example. The outfit she was wearing at MHS that day (tight jeans with a long unbuttoned shirt and a turban) would not have been acceptable there. She also described it as a school that emphasizes religion through emphasis on behavior and strict policy on separation of the sexes.[22] More research needs to be done on these in the future.

Notes

1. http://www.ecolelaplume.com/blog.
2. Philippe Grenier opened in 2016, it is located five minutes away from La Plume.
3. In terms of number of years, elementary school in France lasts 5 years (versus 6 in the US) and starts with 1st grade (CP), KG corresponds to the last year of preschool. Typically, public elementary and preschools in France are separate and in different buildings.
4. A post shows a picture of seven men: the founders of Eva de Vitray and the president of the association that oversees the only primary school under contract at the time, Medersa Tarlimoul Islam in La Réunion. Here are the comments that followed (dated January 2015): Person A: Where is Eva? Only sons of Adam... Eva de Vitray: Yet without Eva, no Adam, no school... Person B: And above all, no children...
5. https://www.nouvelobs.com/societe/20170120.OBS4088/ecole-les-parents-musulmans-sont-des-parents-francais-comme-les-autres.html.
6. http://www.ecole-evadevitray.fr/ and https://www.facebook.com/Evadevitray.fr/.
7. http://www.deendeconfiance.com/lycee-meo-high-school-1er-lycee-a-ethique-musulmane-a-paris/.
8. The CPE, who was a monitor in a high school located in a ZEP, was struck when she realized one day that a 10th grader couldn't read the time.
9. http://meohighschool.org/. Consulted on 13 March 2018.
10. https://www.societe.com/societe/meoplus-groupe-811514652.html.
11. Usually in English this saying is rendered as: "The best gift from a Father to his child is education and upbringing" but I am translating literally the French that was used: "Jamais un père n'a fait à son enfant meilleur présent qu'une bonne éducation."
12. The part about Averroès focuses on its link with the UOIF and the controversial speakers it has invited. Two testimonies from former members of the UOIF explain how they were recruited, and the plan to Islamize French society through the youth. The journalist's voice-over sums up that the UOIF opened Averroes in order to «form this youth and prepare them to infiltrate the spheres of power » "formater cette jeunesse [d'Averroes] et la préparer à infiltrer les sphères du pouvoir." The goal is to form an elite that will hold key posts in the government and society, including in the media, higher education, medicine, law, and hospitals to implement a communitarist society. They asked to film in Averroès but were not granted access.
13. I contacted the city hall and Stéphane Gatignon repeatedly to interview him, with no response, and as luck would have it, on the day I went to

the city hall to try to meet with him, he had just turned in his resignation that morning.
14. See the following articles for reactions from the school (Brancato) and Gatignon (Toussay) to the documentary.
15. http://hudhud.biz/?q=school/el-dirayah-apcs.html.
16. Unless there was a confusion with another school, which happened in the case of La Fraternité, which she told me was not an official school since no declaration of opening had been filed with the city, which is unlikely since the school is registered in the Academy.
17. http://associationamana.wixsite.com/associationamana/contact.
18. www.amana-education.fr.
19. This news segments aired on France 2, but I couldn't find the date. https://www.youtube.com/watch?v=4nwirCXjPMY.
20. https://www.fort-school.com/. Accessed on 8 March 2018.
21. https://www.youtube.com/watch?v=4nwirCXjPMY.
22. When I tried to visit that school, I observed a dozen girls playing ping pong and eating pizza under the supervision of a man during lunch time. It boasts a pass rate of 91% for the 2018 middle school exam and 100% for ES track and 95% for S track for the high school exam. The CPE could not speak with me, but assured me that she would give my information to the director who was out with one class at a field trip for a week. I never heard back and follow-up emails went unanswered.

References

Bastide, Emmanuelle, and Charlie Dupiot. «Être musulman en France.» *7 Milliards De Voisins Podcast: RFI*, 4 March 2015. http://www.rfi.fr/emission/20150304-etre-musulman-france.

Bey, Nadia. «Voies de Femmes.» *Radio Orient*, 30 June 2016. http://www.radioorient.com/wp-content/uploads/2016/07/Voies-de-Femmes-lyc%C3%A9e-%C3%A9thique-musulmane-30062016.mp3.

Billon, Annick, et al. «Rapport Fait au nom de la commission de la culture, de l'éducation et de la communication sur la proposition de loi visant à simplifier et mieux encadrer le régime d'ouverture des établissements privés hors contrat.» 7 February 2018. http://www.senat.fr/rap/l17-277/l17-2771.pdf.

Brancato, Rémi. «A Sevran, 10 jours après "Dossier Tabou": "on souffre de cette image-là".» *France Bleu*, 10 October 2016. https://www.francebleu.fr/infos/societe/sevran-10-jours-apres-dossier-tabou-souffre-de-cette-image-la-1475868353.

Bras, J.-P., S. Mervin, S. Amghar, L. Fournier, O. Marongiu, and B. Godard. "L'enseignement de l'Islam dans les écoles coraniques les institutions de formation islamique et les écoles privées." Rapport du IISMM &

EHESS, 2010. http://www.disons.fr/wp-content/uploads/2012/03/RAPPORTENSEIGNEMENT-ISLAMIQUE-final.pdf.

Hargreaves, Alec. "A Deviant Construction: The French Media and the *Banlieues*." *Journal of Ethnic and Migration Studies* 22.4 (October 1996): 607–618.

Heidsieck, Louis. « Le lycée « universaliste » MHS lance un appel aux dons. » *Le eFigaro*, 1 February 2017.

Laurence, Jonathan, and Justin Vaisse. *Integrating Islam in France: Political and Religious Challenges in Contemporary France*. Washington, DC: Brookings Institution Press, 2006.

La Villardière, Bernard de. *L'islam en France: la République en échec*. 28 septembre 2016.

Puzenat, Amélie. *Conversions à l'islam*. Rennes: Presses Universitaires de Rennes, 2015.

Toussay, Jade. « Le maire de Sevran accuse Bernard de la Villardière de "jeter de l'huile sur le feu" avec "Dossier Tabou". » *Huffpost*, 29 September 2016. https://www.huffingtonpost.fr/2016/09/29/dossier-tabou-sevran-stephane-gatignon-reaction_n_12249484.html.

Vitray-Meyerovitch, Eva de, Rachel Cartier, and Jean-Pierre Cartier. *Islam, l'autre visage: entretiens avec Rachel et Jean-Pierre Cartier*. Paris: Criterion, 1991.

CHAPTER 6

Arabic and Islamic Studies

PART I: DEVALUING OF ARAB-MUSLIM CULTURE IN PUBLIC SCHOOLS

Social Class and Education

Recent results from the PISA studies show that France has one of the most elitist educational systems in the world, with one of the widest gaps between the performance of students from privileged and underprivileged backgrounds (Chaar). There are many factors that can explain the high rate of academic failure seen in some neighborhoods. In the case of many children of immigrants, Keaton adds to the social class handicap the following factors:

> [...] parents who have had little formal schooling, … substandard education and social stigma, …failure to diagnose students' academic (and emotional) difficulties early, … overcrowded classes in core subjects, and a lack of resources, will, and know-how in treating students who do not respond to a teacher-centered, transmission-response pedagogical approach that requires all students to master the same knowledge at the same time. (141)

Pierre Bourdieu has written at length in several landmark studies about how the French educational system legitimates the social order, and the key role it plays in maintaining and reproducing the social divide between the elites, who are overrepresented in the most prestigious

© The Author(s) 2019
C. Bourget, *Islamic Schools in France*,
https://doi.org/10.1007/978-3-030-03834-2_6

schools and tracks, and the underprivileged. Because the gap between the cultural capital transmitted at school and the lower classes narrows as one climbs up the social ladder, privileged students, for whom the cultural capital passed on at home and at school are very close, have a head start. The school system and its hierarchy of prestige maintain the ruling class' hold on the most prestigious degree-granting institutions while the role played by social class and cultural capital remains hidden under the pretense of meritocracy ("Reproduction culturelle" 58). It then legitimizes these inequalities by attributing them to students' merit instead of cultural heritage, and legitimates its transmission by "dissimulating the fact that it performs this function" (Bourdieu and Passeron 210). In *Reproduction in Education*, the notion of cultural capital is only problematized through the category of social classes. When Bourdieu talks about cultural capital, it is within the broad framework of French culture with a class differentiation: the culture taught in school is close to the ruling class' culture, but far from the middle class' culture and farther still from the lower class' one. But other factors which are not as easily measurable as social class might also be having an impact.

Devaluation of Arab-Muslim Practice in Education

Bourdieu never considers explicitly that the gap is even wider for minorities who hail from a foreign, non-Western cultural heritage. In *The Weight of the World*, he refers to culturally disadvantaged students, by which is meant working class and/or of foreign origin (492), but there is no single mention of the issue of Islam as a particular marker of stigmatization and disenfranchisement in the entire book.[2] Islam is brought up in the context of K-12 education only once: a school director recalls that during the 1990–1991 school year, when riots erupted in various disadvantaged areas, his middle school did not see any agitation during Ramadan; he then presents as evidence that the school is located in a "very distinguishable" neighborhood the fact that on Eid celebration only 160 out of 420 students attended school (*The Weight* 495). But he does not go on to consider the implications of this particular "distinction" which is clearly linked to Islamic practices.

Attention needs to be paid not only to social class but also to the effect of cultural heritage on educational outcomes in France, such as the effect that ambient Islamophobia can have on Muslim students, especially when some of it trickles into the school, and when some educators display hostility and suspicion. On an obvious level, this Islamophobia comes in the form of objections to different degrees of students trying to observe some of their faith practices and rituals. These have ranged from the exclusion of veiled girls to teachers pressuring students to not fast during Ramadan because it "was detrimental to their health and depleted their energy, thereby jeopardizing their grades" (Keaton 147). Dupaire and Mabilon point out that decisions such as cancelling alternative meals "fuel conflicts that have no basis and prompt Muslims to take charge of their children's schooling" (87). There are some accommodations done on a school-by-school basis: for instance, some schools do reimburse families for lunch not eaten at the cafeteria during Ramadan, but not all agree to do that (Lorcerie 2010: 66).

Some parents have mentioned this hardening climate as a reason for taking their children out of the public system. Puzenat lists the following complaints against public schools in her study[3]: the double standard that is most obvious through the Christmas celebrations while outlawing the Muslim headscarf, the difficulties encountered by parents who do not want their children to eat meat at school while fish is served on Fridays[4] (Puzenat 220–222), etc. I heard many similar complaints during my visits, as well as women not allowed to chaperone field trips because of their headscarves, aggravations from teachers when parents do not want their children to eat the non-halal cafeteria meat, etc. I was told about a preschool girl who came home crying one day because a whole drama ensued when she refused to eat meat at school: the teacher saying that the girl needed to eat meat to get a balanced nutrition, the mother countering that the child ate meat at home at night and on the weekend and there were no dietary deficiencies in her diet. While some might dismiss this incident as trivial, it was perceived by mother and child as a clear form of harassment. Other anecdotes narrated to me include children told by other children that their mother forbade them to play with them because their mothers were veiled. Some women avoid going to some appointments so as to not bring prejudice to their husbands and children. One observed that there is a lot more tolerance for Orthodox Jews.

I was told about a mother who moved nearly 400 miles away so her children could attend a Muslim school, after being barred from entering her children's public school because of her scarf. She now volunteers at the school and teaches Arabic, she is also the president of an interfaith association, because it means a lot to her to show that we can live together despite differences. There are many testimonies about the emotional toll the headscarf affair had on veiled girls, so it is fair to surmise that these other issues are causing frustrations and resentment not only among parents, but also among students.

Promoting a national culture common to all has been a main function of public schools, and Muslims in France are not the first to see their culture barred from it. In the past, the French nation-building project has come at the detriment of regional languages in France, and of native languages and cultures in the colonies. In France, this suppression was followed by grass-root revivalism of regional cultures and languages in the 1980s, to the point that the current weight and pressure exercised by regional languages schools is disproportionate with their number according to the Ministry of Education. Keaton pointed out that "very little substantive change has occurred as a result of their presence [of Muslim youth] in French public schools" and that "If anything, the system has rigidified" (99). The assumption is still that students should adapt to the system and not the other way around (Ferrara 2012: 515). As Keaton noted when analyzing the issue of the Muslim background in female students' secondary education:

> In many respects, to be Muslim in France and in secular institutions can be a difficult obligation to fulfil, especially when attempting to maintain a cultural equilibrium between expected behaviour (e.g., fasting, praying, dressing modestly) and the realities of work and school in which such practices are deemed disruptive or unacceptable in secular public space. This is especially true for those girls who practice or want to publicly display their understanding of Islam. (146)

Unfortunately, the French State's stance has been leaning toward the extreme of excluding every practice linked to Islam, while some schools do show that some accommodations are possible without jeopardizing the goal of educating all students into a national culture.

Devaluation of Arab-Muslim Culture in Teaching Practices and Curriculum

Obstacles to practicing some aspects of the Muslim religion are compounded by the symbolic devaluation of its culture and heritage, which few researchers have addressed as a religion and not ethnicity. Even when educators have a benign or benevolent attitude, there are structural features in the system that contribute to the devaluation of students' cultures of origins, and that can play a direct or indirect role on performance in school. Durpaire and Mabilon-Bonfils point to a dual social and cultural handicap for children who belong to both lower class and are of Maghrebian origin (61). Studies tabulating first names in high school sections confirm the ethnic segregation of high school tracks, with Muslim names overrepresented in the least prestigious ones (55). More studies are needed about the effects on students success (or lack thereof) of having their home culture systematically denigrated.

Research shows how the national curriculum can conflict with some of the values taught at home. Keaton details some of the issues in the curriculum, such as sexual education in Natural Sciences courses and participating in co-ed swimming lessons during PE (149)[5]; Bowen looks at how a Muslim school handled teaching Darwin's theory of evolution in biology and same-sex unions in Civics (2010).[6] In the wake of the headscarf affairs, many deplored the absence of religion (as an object of studies) in the curriculum. Durpaire and Mabilon-Bonfils add the absence of African history in the curriculum, and point out the numerous stereotypes and prejudices about Islam (65–80). Their analysis of the word Islam in textbooks used in 2015 showed that most references were to conflicts, particularly radicalization and terrorism with 9/11 and the headscarf affair in France (71–79).

The national curriculum is very Franco-centric in some subjects, and teaches "to be French with the implicit understanding that French culture is superior to the cultures that they are presumed to have" (Keaton 97), particularly in subjects like history and French literature where the national project comes to bear (Keaton 91). Indeed, "History, like French literature, plays a fundamental role in shaping youths' self-understandings by structuring their collective memory of events and facts in a way that contributes to making them French citizens, invested with the ideals of France" (Keaton 116). Looking at the French subject, Keaton found that even in schools where there was a large and visible presence of students of African origins, the majority of teachers (who appeared to be of European origin) stuck to the French literary cannon and that 94% of the literature taught was by French writers of European descent, despite a large body of literature from Francophone writers from the African continent, and even when test preparation was not a constraining factor in the selection of books (113–114). Keaton cites a study by

Manesse and Grellet who found that "teachers still preferred literature written by authors whose heritage reflected their own, writings that they knew well and felt comfortable using" (114). This points to the slow recognition of Francophone studies as a legitimate academic field in France.

Issues about what is taught and not taught in other subjects matter as well. Jo McCormack has analyzed the teaching of the Algerian War, which has been on the general high school curriculum since 1983. But being on the curriculum and in textbooks does not always guarantee significant attention in classrooms, in part because of time constraints. McCormack concluded that "The marginalization of the Algerian War in the education system, largely due to the divisive nature of the conflict and Republican principles guiding the school system, does encourage ethnic tensions by leaving the field open to rival memories and not providing a segment of the school population with significant elements of its identity" (174). McCormack urges French elites to "recognize the clear link between unresolved memories of the Algerian War and current exclusion along ethnic lines in French society" (182). Keaton comes to the same conclusion about the teaching of colonial history in general, particularly in the wake of the push to legislate an official recognition of the "positive role" of colonization in 2005 (117–121).

Other less obvious examples are all the more pernicious. Keaton notes that "there are real tensions between students and teachers, born of mutual misperceptions and mistrust, which are exacerbated by patterns of inequality and such issues. I am not suggesting that surface incivilities between students and teachers are not an issue, but they are inherent in a dysfunctional educational system that reduces learning to relations of force" (132). These power relations are quite obvious in some accounts of teachers in school. One very popular semi-autobiographical narrative that was turned into a film is replete with such examples. *Entre les murs* shows the cultural gap that teachers are unable or unwilling to bridge, particularly when it comes to minorities, and most importantly, their lack of awareness of it. In one example, the French teacher is taken to task by his students for always using French and American first names in the model sentences he gives (32), whereas the majority of his class has "foreign" names (and a good number of them clearly Muslim names), thus excluding his (Muslim) students from the realm of examples of standard

French. In addition, Durpaire and Mabilon-Bonfils question seemingly benevolent practices particularly prevalent in primary grades such as the "couscous projects," which asks students about culinary traditions, arts and crafts from the countries of origin. They argue that cultures of origins are excluded from the daily routine but exhibited as folklore a couple of hours a month, thereby participating in othering some students (26).

In an article asking tongue-in-cheek whether there were Muslim students in French schools (following a statement from the Ministry of Education that there were no Muslim students), Lorcerie insists that it must be asked and more importantly answered, despite the fact that it is easier to ignore it because of the shift it would entail on the part of the Ministry of Education and society at large regarding its secular and meritocratic stance. Lorcerie forcefully argues that it is important for Muslims to be accepted as Muslims in schools, that teachers and staff must be trained accordingly, and that silence on the issue is no longer tenable (Lorcerie 2012: 70). Students who have gone to Muslim schools claimed in interviews conducted post-high school graduation "that the familial environment, the lack of discrimination or feelings of being ostracized, and the dedication of the teachers all boosted their confidence, ability to learn, and for many, their academic success" (Ferrara 2018: 21). All these shortcomings from the public system highlight the needs that Muslim schools might fill.

Part II: Arabic and Islam in Muslim Schools

While some teachers gave me permission to use their names, I decided not to in order to better protect the anonymity of those who requested it. In this section, I am omitting also school names for two reasons: to better ensure anonymity, and also because similarities overpowered differences. The diversity in terms of teaching styles and focus existed within schools and not between schools. For instance, the religion teachers I found the most effective at engaging students about being French and Muslims were all teaching in different schools. I use the word religion for convenience to designate classes focused on Islam, but I must stress that all schools purposefully use different terms to designate them, as detailed in previous chapters.

Ambiance

According to the 2010 report, religion classes are not the main criteria for the Islamic character of these schools, but their ambiance. What contributes to this atmosphere are the following facts: there is a prayer room and some teachers do pray, many female teachers wear a headscarf, Muslim holidays are celebrated (with schools closing on the Eids), and some (not all) even close on Friday afternoons to allow attending the weekly Friday prayers at the mosque (Bras et al. 48). This Muslim environment constitutes one main appeal for parents, who take comfort in the fact that they are (in theory) sheltered from a permissive society (Bras et al. 48). The school becomes a surrogate that replaces other structures that are no longer there, such as village, family, etc. (Bras et al. 48).

When I asked students what their main motivation was to come to their specific school, students mentioned the headscarf, religion classes, and the academic level. When I asked what the advantage was to be in a Muslim school, answers included being able to practice their religion, particularly wearing the veil, the possibility to pray, and being able to express themselves freely. One student mentioned that "when we speak people understand you." Arabic has references to God embedded in many commonly used expressions in daily life (inshallah, for instance). Some Muslims (whether they speak Arabic or not) sprinkle these Arabic phrases more or less liberally when they speak, and in their school, everybody understands them, but when they are among non-Muslims, sometimes such a phrase will slip out and they feel the need to watch what they say.

Arabic and Islamic Studies are the two classes that distinguish the curriculum of Muslim schools from public schools. These subjects contribute greatly to making these schools do more than provide an "Islamic ambiance through religious practice and celebrations" (Bowen 2010: 124).

Arabic

Arabic is not just a heritage language for many (but not all) Muslim French. It has a privileged place in Islam, as it is the language in which the Scriptures were revealed. It is used by all practicing Muslims on a daily basis when reciting prayers, whether they have any proficiency in the language or not. The Qur'an is considered as a miracle and as the word of God, and any translation from Arabic is considered as just that:

a translation. That is why virtually all Muslim schools offer Arabic as a foreign language. One parent of Amazigh ancestry I spoke with did not see a need for Arabic, but that is a minority view among Muslim parents enrolling their children in a Muslim school.

According to Gharrafi, the teaching of Arabic in France in secondary schools mirrors its failed policies of immigration (131). While it goes back to the seventeenth century, and the two national competitive exams to recruit teachers were instituted in 1906 and 1975, three centuries later, it is lagging behind other languages because of the sizeable presence of Arab immigrants in France. The ELCO or Teachings of the Language and Culture of Origin (enseignements de langue et de culture d'origine) were set up in the 1970s with Algeria, Morocco, Tunisia, Turkey, Spain, Portugal, Italy, and Yugoslavia to help children of immigrants who would eventually go home. Classes were taught by teachers appointed and paid by the countries of origin without any control from the French government. This program contributed to marginalizing Arabic (Ghouati).

When the Ministry of Education announced that it was going to reform the teaching of Arabic in 2016 by phasing out the ELCO and introduce Arabic in first grade, reactions were quick. Representative Annie Genevard qualified Arabic as a "langue communautaire" "communitarian language" whose teaching would foster "the *communautarisme* that sap national cohesion" (Peyronie 10). The reform's goal is to transform a language such as Arabic from a language of origin into a foreign language. Gharrafi deplores that Arabic is reduced to identity politics, and the poor response of the National Education which is to hold off and reluctantly open Arabic classes in public schools for fear that they will foster *communautarisme* (127–128).

In 2006, there were 5500 students taking Arabic in secondary schools and 1800 studying it through distance learning via the CNED which shows that there is an unmet demand (Gharrafi 128). Enrollment increased, and Poucet gives two different numbers: 7300 secondary students studying Arabic in 2008 (*La liberté* 202), and 7000 in 2010 ("Naissance" 1967), in both cases pointing out that these numbers are half the numbers of the 1970s. As a comparison, Poucet notes that 30,000 students studied Chinese in 2010. For the 2016–2017 school year, numbers for languages taught showed (in decreasing order): English (far ahead), Spanish, German, Italian, Chinese, regional languages (combined), Portuguese, and Arabic (ahead of Russian by

42 students).[7] As several reports and studies have shown, there is a very strong demand for Arabic, but it is not met by the public schools (Ghouati). One estimate states that the numbers of students studying Arabic in mosques have increased tenfold in the past twenty years (Durand). The latest numbers for 2017–2018 show 567 students studying Arabic in elementary public schools, and 11,174 in secondary schools, which is fewer than Chinese (Durand). There has been a lack of job security for Arabic teachers due to lack of support from the Ministry. Given the decrease in support by the Ministry for the teaching of Arabic and the increased demand as evidenced by enrollment in local associations and higher education (Ghouati), Muslim private schools, which all offer Arabic, are meeting another need than just private education.

According to Mamèche, there are only two to three inspectors employed by the Ministry of Education for Arabic language for the entire country. If there is a stronger demand (as the increase in Muslim schools seems to forecast), the Ministry will have to step up (Interview September 2016). Most families in Muslim schools want their children to learn Arabic, except those who speak it at home and thus prefer that their children study a different language. There is another factor that affects the choice of Arabic (versus other languages): whether it is offered in competitive *grandes écoles* or not, which might affect students' higher education prospects (Interview with a Principal 2016). Some public school principals do not want Arabic offered in their school for fear of attracting a stigmatized student population (Ghouati 114).

Most Arabic teachers I spoke with had a Bachelor's degree, some a Master's, and one was ABD (DEA in Arabic). One teacher's situation is an example of what happens when a school is only partially under contract, since contracts are granted one class at a time in most cases. This teacher had 8 hours of his teaching under contract with the state, for the remaining 10 hours he had a CDI, a type of temporary, low-paid contract that was set up to reduce unemployment, particularly among youth. According to him, there are only about three to four positions available nationwide each year for the Arabic CAPEPS, the national recruiting exam for private schools under contract. In the public system, 18 hours a week is considered full time, whereas in the private, it is 24 hours a week.

The textbooks used by the schools follow the Common European Framework of Reference for Languages (CEFR) scale for proficiency to teach foreign languages; they include the following (each textbook was used in more than one school):

- *Ahdâf:* a partnership between the IMA (Institute of the Arab World) and Didier editions.
- *Kullu tamâm*: written under the supervision of an Academy inspector, with professors from renowned schools such as Lycée Henri IV and Honoré de Balzac International school.
- *Ouhib allugha al arabiyya* and other series for different levels from the same publisher JSF (Editions Jeunesse sans frontières 2007). This book has some religious references in the publication date following the Hijra calendar next to the Christian one and the Bismillah that starts the introduction. Other series include *Ouhibou al arabiyya wa ataalamouha* (2015), and *Al arabiyyah lalchabaab.*

Many teachers and administrators I spoke with felt that there was a lot of room for improvement of Arabic textbooks, and said that they use supplementary materials. One Arabic teacher said that the textbook recommended by the Ministry of Education includes some North African dialect because they assume that children have dialectal Arabic at home, which is not the case for the vast majority of students (80% according to her). A couple of teachers did not use textbooks: one developed her own materials, the other used handouts passed on from the Arabic teacher at the Lycée Henri IV. The FNEM is in the process of developing a program, but it takes time.

One school had some issues with the intertwining of Arabic and religion, in part because given the fact that the Qur'an is in Arabic, it is easy to integrate religion in an Arabic language class and vice versa. The Arabic inspector from the Academy who came to inspect the year prior to my visit had a lot of criticism about the way they teach Arabic (though as the director complained, she only spent 10 minutes in each class, which is not enough to have an idea about what is done). The director is having ongoing discussions with the teachers to dissociate the religion from the language (by refraining from using Arabic words such as the word *salat*). A preschool class I observed shows how it is pedagogically sound and easy to integrate Arabic and religious classes at that level and thus all the more difficult to negotiate a clear separation in the context of a Muslim school. Moreover, a complete purging of religion might render the Arabic language taught culturally inauthentic. The issue of clearly separating Arabic and religion came up in some of the other schools in a different way, with teachers insisting on using French equivalents to Arabic words such as Allah in religion classes.

Most of the classes I observed followed the communicative method, with the class conducted in the target language as much as possible. I saw a full range of teaching competencies during those visits, from a teacher unable to handle basic class management issues (the only one), to excellent and outstanding teachers (the vast majority) with very impressive results in some schools in terms of students' speaking and listening skills (I could only judge oral and aural skills based on students' satisfactory answers to their teachers). One of the biggest challenges (common to all classes) is to have groups of different abilities, something several schools are addressing by splitting up classes into two groups of one higher level and one lower.

Sample of Arabic Class Observations
In an effort to give a sense of what happens in a typical Arabic class in Muslim schools in France, here are brief summaries of some of the classes I observed, from different schools and levels.

High School: 10th Grade Arabic LVII (2nd Foreign Language), 13 Students
The class was conducted entirely in Arabic and followed a task-based method. Students had a handout about the history of Syria, the Omeyyade dynasty, and the Omeyyade mosque. The teacher went over exercises with questions about the history of Andalusia and its dynasties. This was in preparation for an assignment that the students had been given, which consisted in recording a presentation of the mosque as if it were to be an audio guide. They had a detailed handout with scaffolding tasks and resources (written and video, but also maps and pictures). In the course of the history summary, the teacher recapitulated the history of the califs prior to Mu'awiyya, and few of them knew all first four Righteously-guided califs (I expected more students in a Muslim school would know that).

Middle School: 6th Grade Arabic, 14 Students
The teacher spoke Arabic most of the time. One student wrote the date on the board, then the whole class recited the alphabet. Students were called on to write some letters on the board. Two students read a dialogue in the textbook. The teacher asked questions to verify comprehension of the dialogue, then gave a brief explanation of a grammar rule. There were many different levels of proficiency in this class with some

students reading very well and others struggling, but overall all students participated well.

Elementary: 5th Grade Arabic, 11 Students
These students get 5 hours of Arabic every week, taught in half groups. The teacher spoke in Arabic at all times, asking students various questions which they answered easily, and they understood and answered everything. The teacher asked what they were going to do during the break (this was the last day of school before Spring break), one said he would visit his family in Tunisia and another one in Morocco. After reading a dialogue in the book and answering comprehension questions, they started reviewing various grammar points and vocabulary in quick succession (conjugation, possessives, family vocabulary), and also the names of the planets in Arabic, as a preparation for an upcoming five-day field trip to Cap Astro. They ended with a song and wrote their homework in Arabic.

Preschool: First Year, 7 Children
These children get 2 hours of Arabic per day: one hour in the morning and one in the afternoon, but this was the beginning of their exposure since the school year had barely started. All of them had Arabic first names except for one. Some of the Arabic names were pronounced in a French way, thus a little boy named Khaled was called Kaled, because as the teacher informed me, this is what he is used to.[8] The majority of children in that school did not have Arabic at home. The teacher introduced daily vocabulary little by little. She started with some TPR (getup, sit down), then proceeded with introductions. Children learned various phrases about their daily class routine: wash your hands, snack, good job, thank you, and religious phrases often used such as mashaAllah, inshallah, and bismillah in the context of having their snack. The teacher proceeded with an activity to teach three colors in Arabic, with cards, followed by a song about the Arabic alphabet, focusing on the first four letters.

Preschool: Third Year, 14 Children
Arabic teaching happened in the context of snack time, and we can see here how the language and religion (more specifically Islamic manners in this case) can be easily integrated. They first said a brief supplication in Arabic before eating, then the teacher asked questions in Arabic to name the food they were about to eat, followed by another supplication

after the snack. An activity teaching vocabulary followed, with pictures of a cat and a bear, and each child got a turn to match the picture with the word written in Arabic; then they sang a song about a cat. For the next activity, children made the shape of the Arabic letter *mim* with play-dough. The teacher then told the story of Adam and creation in French. Children talked and asked questions (a little girl asked what taala meant after the teacher used the phrase Allah subhana wa taala, a little boy talked about his deceased grandfather, another one about his father). After a supplication about the Prophet, the class ended with a game of Simon says in Arabic.

Islam

Islamic education can refer to a myriad different things, as evidenced by the collection of articles compiled by Mujadad Zaman and Nadeem Memon. In his introduction to a volume on Islamic knowledge in the West, Van Bruinessen concludes that although complemented by alternative methods, the "classical, madrasa-style mode of transmission continues in Europe" (20). A chapter by Allievi in the same volume contextualizes the theoretical and practical underpinnings of producing Islamic knowledge in Europe, and argues that this process is in a transitional phase. They are speaking about Europe as a whole and all Islamic teachings, most of which probably takes place in the context of weekend schools for school-age students.

The 2010 report on Islamic education in France saw as the main objective for the religion classes to give students the basics of Islam to motivate them to practice the religion, and distinguished three main themes:

- morality (regrouping an eclectic mix including backbiting, family relationships, injustice, anger, self-confidence)
- religious practices (different kinds of prayers)
- topics according to the occasion (hijrah, birth of the prophet, mihraj, Ramadan) (Bras et al. 46–47).

These are still and will likely continue to be a major part of the religious curriculum. However, based on my discussions and observations, it seems that there has been a reorientation and refocusing since the time of the report.

When I asked a couple of religion teachers about influential thinkers on Muslims in France, one mentioned two figures who he found very interesting but who have different approaches. First, Tariq Ramadan as the most covered by the media, who appeared at the opportune time at the right place; he himself in 1995 had not heard Islamic scholars talk about Islam in French. Second, Tareq Oubrou, also an influential figure though newer on the scene. The teacher contrasted both figures as Ramadan being more militant, whereas Oubrou puts more emphasis to adapt to one's context as long as you keep your minimum obligations to your faith. Oubrou is more open to conciliations with the political system, so, for instance, he says that in France, wearing the scarf is not compulsory. In a chapter dedicated to reforming Islamic education, Tariq Ramadan advocates for a contextualized religious education, and to study the Qur'an and Prophet's life in concert with students' lives (257). This seems to be the guiding principle for all schools. Another teacher mentioned activists fighting Islamophobia, such as the director of the CCIF (Collectif contre l'islamophobie en France). Another teacher, whose goal is to secularize religion, made reference to the Moatazila and to Edgar Morin's book *L'Education du futur*.

Another common point I heard from most schools: religion classes were definitely not the main concern.[9] Opening a school and most importantly funding it is a huge undertaking, and the priority in the beginning for all schools was academic excellence in the subjects mandated by the national curriculum. For the most part, students do not get evaluated in religion classes. None of the religion classes I visited used a textbook. About half of the teachers relied on handouts they created or pieced together, and the rest just did a mix of lecture and guided conversation. Several teachers and administrators noted that now that the necessary stability has been achieved (at least for some schools who are fully/partially under contract), it is time to devote resources to this effort. When I spoke with Mamèche in 2016, he said that it was one of the FNEM's priority. A new book that targets 5- to 6-year olds (CP or K-1st grade) titled *Islam, fondements, valeurs et pratiques* has just been co-published with the FNEM. In the description by the publisher, the book combines secular and religious teachings; it has been "designed to form a future French citizen of Muslim faith" and addresses interfaith issues linked to modern science and national belonging. One of the authors of this book is Fatila Ould Saïd, who teaches at Samarcande.[10]

Teachers' backgrounds varied and included people who had emigrated from Morocco and Algeria, as well as native French. Some of the teachers were very charismatic and really knew how to catch students' attention, with a conversational style, familiar phrasing, and a good sense of humor. Most of them (with a couple of exceptions) sprinkled Arabic religious phrases liberally such as insha Allah, and a common blessing (sallalla aleihu wa sallam) after the prophet's name. They used both the French Dieu and Allah to refer to God, with the exception of one teacher who systematically corrected students when they used the word Allah by reminding them to use the word "Dieu" "God." Teachers were clearly passionate about their subject matter.

During most of the lessons I observed, the majority of students were very engaged, attentive, and participated. They were not hesitant to answer and ask questions, and many classes were quite lively. Some classes made systematic connections with the students' immediate context, be it about fulfilling one's religious obligation or the news. As Ferrara observed, schools "lean toward a universal and inclusive interpretation of Islam" (2018: 17), emphasizing "the respect with which people of other faiths must be treated" (2018: 18). In the classes I observed, there was a mix of traditional education and adaptation to a new context. There was attention given to the Scriptures, with memorization and explanation of the Qur'an, an important aspect of traditional Muslim education and practice, but also how to live by its core tenets as twenty-first-century French citizens, including taking care of oneself and our natural environment and people, relationships with others and how to address moral dilemmas and controversial issues, including Islamic terrorism, euthanasia, organ donations, and interest on loans. Teachers focused on values central to Islam such as balance, honesty, and charity. I include below a summary of the content of lessons given by different teachers in different schools, again not identifying the specific titles of the classes nor the schools to better guarantee the request for anonymity by some.

Sample of "Muslim Religion" Class Observations
Elementary: K-1st Grade, 26 Students
The class started with a supplication (*du'a*), then students sang a song about the prophet Mohammed, with the Arabic lyrics written on the board. The teacher then asked students to summarize the story of the shepherd that she had told them the preceding class and asked for

the moral of the story (that we are not allowed to give something that does not belong to us). The teacher stressed the importance of respecting others by telling the truth. She then explained another hadith about a woman who wanted to mix water in milk to earn more money, but her daughter spoke against it and Omar Ibn al-Khattab married her for her honesty. Children colored a drawing illustrating the hadith.

Elementary: 5th Grade, 12 Students
This class focused mostly on recitation (a discipline in itself in Islamic Sciences), with a few explanations of the content. The teacher spoke in Arabic the whole time, students seemed to understand but answered in French. The class started with each student reading one verse of the Qur'an, with the teacher correcting some pronunciation (for some of the letters that do not have equivalents in French such as *qaf*). Then students recited/read while following the recitation playing on a tape. The teacher told me she uses tapes of Sheikh al-Fassi because she does not have a nice voice but he recites clearly and slowly. One of the girls was very noticeably swaying while reciting, and her facial expression as well as another girl's clearly displayed some deep emotional connection to the recitation. The class then reviewed the five pillars of Islam with the names in Arabic and translation in French. The teacher explained that the pillars are only 5% of the religion, the remaining 95% consist in *husn lkhuluq*, which she defined as the behavior with your parents, neighbors, etc. The class ended with a supplication for the Prophets Mohammed and Ibrahim.

Middle School: 6th Grade, 9 Students (Half of a Class)
The lesson started by following up on an optional assignment which consisted of filling out a chart on a calendar to try to improve one's behavior and habits. After the teacher stressed how difficult it is to change bad habits, one student volunteered to show his chart. Then one student summarized the story of Abil and Qabil which they read last time and asked questions about envy and jealousy, and the need to control oneself and one's emotions. The teacher stressed that incest is strictly forbidden and was only allowed once at that particular time in order for humanity to develop.

Then the teacher distributed a text, and asked about the definition of the word "faillite" which students answered as losing all material possessions. The teacher then asked students to contrast their definition with the Prophet's in what is considered an authentic hadith:

> Abu Huraira reported: The Messenger of Allah, peace and blessings be upon him, said, "Do you know who is bankrupt?" They said, "The one without money or goods is bankrupt." The Prophet said, "Verily, the bankrupt of my nation are those who come on the Day of Resurrection with prayers, fasting, and charity, but also with insults, slander, consuming wealth, shedding blood, and beating others. The oppressed will each be given from his good deeds. If his good deeds run out before justice is fulfilled, then their sins will be cast upon him and he will be thrown into the Hellfire.[11]

The teacher drew two columns and distributed the things mentioned under two headings: good deeds (charity, prayer, fast, Qur'an), and bad ones. She explained resurrection, and insisted on the fact that actions that are not sincere are worthless.

She then asked if they had heard the news. Four days prior, on March 23, a car hijacking and hostage situation perpetrated by Radouane Lakdim, acting on behalf of the Islamic State, left five people dead. This attack made headlines for several days as the press hailed the heroism of Lieutenant Colonel Arnaud Beltrame, who was killed after he volunteered to take the place of one of the hostages held in the supermarket (Peltier). The teacher made a parallel between the attacker, who was reported to have shouted "Allahu Akbar," thereby self-identifying as Muslim. She explained that she will not judge whether he is a Muslim or not, but that he has lost whatever good he earned (by maybe praying, reciting Qur'an) by doing evil. One student asked: "doesn't God forgive easily"? The teacher: "God forgives easily for the things that are directed to him, but here the attacker has done harm to others." Going back to the hadith, she asked one child to the board to draw a scale to illustrate the last part of the hadith, taking sanctions, on the one hand, and community service, on the other, as an example relevant to students' reality. She insisted on the fact that relationships with others are not weighed the same as our relationship with God. Following a student comment, she insisted that the police did not kill the terrorist out of revenge, but to ensure he would not cause more casualty, and that whenever they can, the police shoot the legs or arms to disable. When a student pointed out that there are Play Station 4s in prisons (implying that prisoners have it good), the teacher answered that prisoners have to be treated humanely.

Middle School: 7th Grade, 12 Students (Half of a Class)
The teacher started with the story of Abraham and Ismaïl in the Qur'an, in reference to the Eid that had just been celebrated the week before. Here is more or less how the class unfolded as faithfully as I could write down, but not a verbatim rendition:

> *Teacher:* You all know the story of the sacrifice, do you find it weird (bizarre)?

A student asked what he meant by "bizarre;" the teacher rephrased his question by asking if it is normal that God asks someone to kill his son. He pressed on: "Do we have the right to kill someone who is innocent?" Students answered no, the teacher asked: "who said that?"

> *Students:* God.
> *Teacher:* Isn't it contradictory?

Students gave different responses (yes, no as long as it comes from God it's fine).

> *Teacher:* Can God make mistakes? Students: No.
> *Teacher:* God is perfect, therefore he is logical. Does God need us? Students: No.

The teacher then proceeded to a close analysis of some of the Qur'anic verses that relate that well-known story, calling on various students to help by reading and challenging the meaning. When Abraham hears a voice, as the verse goes "do you realize what you have seen in your dream?" which the teacher explained as God asking him "what is happening to you"? "And this is how one rewards those who do good." The teacher interpreted the reward as being the intervening voice. The teacher contended that "And we replaced him with a ram" is a bad translation, because the Arabic *faidnahu* means to liberate someone who has been taken hostage by ransom. In this case, Abraham has been freed from his dream, therefore Eid celebrates the fact that God liberates us from bad thoughts. There was a great atmosphere in the class, students were engaged, listening very attentively, and were quick and comfortable to ask questions. Their reactions ranged from disbelief (this interpretation differs from the mainstream understanding of this episode) to amazement.

Middle School: 7th Grade, 14 Students (Half of a Class)

This class dealt with the pilgrimage and was described to me by the teacher as a class on religious practice, which comprises about 15% of the curriculum only. The teacher had written the following sentence on the board, in French and in Arabic: "Me voici Seigneur, me voici. Tu n'as aucun associé," the litany uttered by pilgrims when they arrive in Mecca. The teacher recapped the main points about the pilgrimage: it is the fifth pillar of Islam (she reminded them of the analogy with a house), and it is compulsory for those who have the means. She brainstormed with students examples of circumstances that would qualify as excuses not to go (sickness, taking care of a baby, work), with a little debate among students ensuing as to whether work is a valid excuse. A student argued that if your boss needs you to work, then you don't have the means to go and are excused. The discussion went a bit off track. Going back to the rituals that must be accomplished during the pilgrimage, the teacher asked the definition of "commemorate." A girl asked about the meaning of throwing stones, the teacher answered by going back to the beginning of the Kaaba.

Middle School: 7th Grade, 28 Students

In the context of mandated interdisciplinary curriculum, several teachers are dealing with food and sleep as topics around the theme of well-being. The teacher started by citing the Qur'an and hadith to show that this is an important topic addressed by both God and the Prophet. A saying advises to fill our stomach with one third food, one third water, and one third air to avoid over-eating. The teacher stressed the balance in Islam in general, and extremes are associated with Satan/Shaytan.

He made a parallelism between spiritual (such as reading Qur'an) and physical nourishment, we should eat to satiate our hunger and target a balance in food and sleep in all aspects in our life. The teacher told the story about three men who informed the Prophet that they were going to fast, pray and remain celibate, to which the prophet answered that he himself was eating, sleeping, and that extremes are not good even in worshipping. The maximum to fast is Prophet David's example and he used to fast every other day. One student asked whether he would also fast when he was sick, followed by another question on fasting and Ramadan. The teacher brought the discussion back on track by insisting that in Islam one should target quality and not quantity. Moreover, he said that one should not forbid oneself the small pleasures in life, and that the Prophet was not constantly talking about God (to which a student exclaimed "astaghfirullah"). A good Muslim is not someone who worships from sunset to sundown.

One student mentioned YouTube: the teacher warned that they should not believe everything they see on YouTube, especially not videos of people who say that if you kill certain people you will go to Paradise. He then returned to conclude on the topic: the purpose of sleep is to repair the human being, body and brain need restorative sleep, night is for sleeping and the day for work.

Middle School: 9th Grade, 27 Students
Class started by stressing the fact that the first sura opens on the mercy of God, a formula (bismillah) that has been trivialized but that is no less extremely powerful. He asked what a sin is, and stressed the complexity of the human being. He defined the word jihad as meaning to make an effort, and explained that those who focus on issues related to what is haram/halal do not understand the message of Islam. He insisted on spirituality, defined as education of the spirit through prayer and fasting. He told them the story of a man who went to talk to Abu Bakr and confided that he was feeling like a hypocrite because he felt spiritual impulses only when he was in the company of the Prophet. The teacher stressed that the Prophet insisted that there is a time for everything, that Allah does not ask us to ignore life. He cited the Qur'an that says "Our Lord, give us in this world [that which is] good and in the Hereafter [that which is] good and protect us from the punishment of the Fire" (2:201), pointing out that the life on earth is mentioned first. He told the story about a companion who spent his time praying. The prophet scolded him by telling him that his body, his family had rights over him, and that one needs to accomplish oneself in this life.

High School: 11th Grade, 11 Students
The teacher started by contrasting a utilitarian moral (which he defined as calculating your benefit: an action is good if it will bring a maximum of pleasure), and a moral of duty which is imperative whatever the situation, and gave the example of school: they come to school even if they don't like to because there will be a professional advantage later on. He then asked: What is Islam's stance? We do certain things out of calculations (for instance, we pray, etc. to go to Paradise, therefore an atheist who gives alms has more merit than a believer). Would our behavior be

the same if it were invisible? A culture of reward is necessary for learning, it is human nature to be attracted by a reward, but we should try to impregnate ourselves with the good, the just, the beautiful, and the love of the just for the sake of it. He then quoted Rawya, a famous Sufi poet. Each person has its nature and Islam adapts: those who do good to earn Paradise and those who go beyond that. The message of Islam is divine but Islam is also human. He gave the example of Omar who put a moratorium on the punishment of cutting the hand of thieves during a time of famine. This (contrary to Kantian morality) shows flexibility, hence the notion of fatwas (legal opinion) because the Qur'an sets up general principles but there is suppleness, for instance, in need, one is allowed to drink a little bit of alcohol to lessen thirst. One big question in France has to do with interest on loans. In the Qur'an, interest is forbidden. Scientists must master their field (not only the text but also the context). One should listen to economists who understand the current economic French context to know that interest today is not the same interest talked about in the Qur'an. Today, in France, a Muslim cannot own some material possession or progress in society without a loan. Abu Hanifa had authorized credit. Money should remain a means and not become an end.

High School: 11th Grade, 22 Students

The teacher reminded the students that the Qur'an is the founding text of Islam, but not all answers are in the Qur'an, so we must use our reason, for example, in the case of euthanasia. Immediately, a student said "haram" "forbidden," and the teacher answered we should think before rushing to a conclusion. He stressed that this is a big debate in France and that Muslims are not participating in the debate. He asked the question: do we have the right in Islam to stop life support? There are two types of euthanasia: active (when a doctor injects something that will entail death), and passive, when one does nothing. The active one is forbidden is Islam (God gives and takes back life, killing is forbidden including suicide). When should death be declared? The brain commands the body so in Islam, death occurs when the brain stops; an encephalogram can be done to declare whether a person is dead. The question of organ donations is authorized by a majority of Islamic scholars based on the verse "who saves a life saves all humankind." He insisted that one needs to go beyond haram/halal. Among issues students will have to face soon are also economic issues, such as loans, for instance, new companies might need loans to get started.

The rest of the lesson was about the scriptures. He went over the list of Holy books: scrolls of Ibrahim, Torah of Moses, Indjil of Issa (the Gospel of Jesus), and Psalms of David. He asked the question as to how the Qur'an was compiled and passed on (scribes wrote down the verses that were then arranged in suras by the Prophet who would recite the entire Qur'an every Ramadan with Djibril). What does the Qur'an talk about? There are three categories of prescriptions: faith, morals, and practice (he insisted that haram/halal are only one part of practice). He listed the five pillars, translated zakat by "purifying social tax" ("impôt social purificateur"). Islam means having a faith, living it from inside, spirituality, and following a practice. A question on ijtihad from a student prompted a brief definition: intellectual effort, and the precision that one must master Arabic to be able to engage in ijtihad. Islam is not just praying. A smile or a good word can be considered alms. To earn paradise, one should spread peace, feed the poor, respect family ties (even if they are not Muslims), and pray (when nobody sees you). Prayer should not be a mechanical habit, but to remember God, fasting is to break with our habits to enter in contact with the divine, zakat is to think of those in need, pilgrimage is to pull oneself from one's environment to go toward Allah, the Creator.

High School: 12th Grade, 19 Students
That lesson was dedicated to fiqh which translates as jurisprudence, though the teacher said that he prefers to use Muslim law since it is a collection of laws. Fiqh is one part of Chari'a (which means the Path, i.e., how to be Muslim). He commented verse III.58 "Dieu vous ordonne de restituer les dépôts à leurs ayants droits." He focused on divine prescriptions, distinguished between what is compulsory (prayers, fast), what is recommended (extra prayers), what is forbidden (alcohol, lying), and what is not recommended and should be avoided (eating with your left hand). Someone asked if women could wear perfume to go to the mosque. The teacher recommended discretion, it is not forbidden but one should be discreet and not empty the bottle, same thing for make-up. The general rule is that if it is not clearly forbidden by an

authentic text, it is allowed. Someone asked if skiing was allowed, to which one student wondered "are there really people like that" (implying silly enough to ask such questions)?

The teacher detailed the branches of fiqh: the cult (prayer, fasting, man to God), and the social domain (relations man to man), one must reference the texts but especially reason; as an example, he said that one should participate in the elections of the country where one lives; 9/10 of the Qur'an is about spirituality and relationships between Muslims and non-Muslims. Only 3–4% talks about legal issues (250 verses only on haram/halal questions out of more than six thousand). When the texts do not mention a specific issue, scholars must do ijtihad (reason and intellectual effort).

Conclusion

Many oppose Muslim (and other faith-based) schools because they strongly believe in a unified public system. As Gasol situates his comments on the current dual French system in the context of concerns about national identity, he wonders about a public service that could have an internal diversity because "if starting from school, we don't put people who have different sensibilities, opinions, and origins, we are not creating the conditions for tomorrow's national unity." His point is well taken, but what he and many others have failed to address is that the public school system has all but been open to differences, and in the case of Muslim students, has greatly contributed to accentuating stigmatization.

Keaton contrasts some classes such as Natural Sciences where there were conflicts between what the school taught and the home culture of some Muslim girls, with Arabic class which provided solace:

> There, students are not merely learning language, they are being exposed to cultural frames beyond the dry dates and facts typically given (or omitted) in their history course. In this class, the majority of the students excelled academically, having grades well above twelve on a twenty point scale. In this class, they had that "x" in their self-representations validated in ways that they did not experience either in their other courses or outside of school. However, Arabic is not among the living languages valued in the selection process for higher education in France. Rather, this role is reserved for German and English. (154)

While Muslim schools teach the dominant culture, they do make room for the minority culture not only in the daily space of the school where it can be practiced but also in its curriculum. Further studies need to be done to establish how much it helps students to assimilate the dominant culture and see themselves as legitimate recipients.

Notes

1. Arabic is offered in a few public schools as a foreign language.
2. Bourdieu talks about stigmatization in general in several of his books, but not about Islam specifically in the French context.
3. While her study focuses on a small segment of the Muslim population, that is, those who have converted to Islam (estimates range from 50–60 thousands), those concerns have been expressed by the wider Muslim population as well (Puzenat 19).
4. Even though Paul VI's changes in penance laws abrogated the abstinence from meat on Fridays in 1966 (hence the French custom of eating fish on that day), the custom of serving fish on Fridays in school cafeterias persisted well beyond the 1980s and into the twenty-first century.
5. As noted in Chapter 5, one Muslim school insists on co-ed swimming lessons, which reflects that not all issues are problematic for all Muslims.
6. After observing classes in civics, biology, and religion, Bowen noted that "the three subject matters lead these three teachers in different directions, but they present their subjects in ways that emphasize an ethical distance between the believer's source of certainty (scripture) and the particular norms or teachings that characterize French society. For the teachers of biology and civics, this ethical stance means that the teacher presents the curriculum as an external set of claims to be learned for specific purposes" (123). In the case of biology, the teacher taught the theory of evolution while pointing out that science is always evolving and this theory could be replaced in the future, the civics class taught about (gay) civil unions as a French law that is not found in Arab-Muslim societies. "The teachers' main concern is to impart knowledge that France requires—about biology, or civics, or for that matter English and history—without giving up an independent religious stance" (*Can Islam* 123–124).
7. See http://cache.media.education.gouv.fr/file/2017/07/7/depp-RERS-2017_902077.pdf, page 114.
8. There is no equivalent in the French language for the "kh" sound.
9. Even in one well-established school, one student, when I asked whether the religious/ethical aspect was beneficial, mentioned that the ethics class taught him a lot, while another said that it was a repetition every year.

10. http://www.mizane.info/quelle-education-musulmane-pour-les-enfants-du-xxie-siecle/.
11. Source: Ṣaḥīḥ Muslim 258.1: https://abuaminaelias.com/dailyhadithonline/2011/05/08/do-you-know-who-the-bankrupt-are/.

References

Bégaudeau, François. *Entre les murs*. Paris: Gallimard, 2006.
Bourdieu, Pierre. «Reproduction culturelle et reproduction sociale.» *Social Science Information/Information sur Les Sciences Sociales* 10.2 (April 1971): 45–79.
Bourdieu, Pierre, and Jean-Claude Passeron. *Reproduction in Education, Society and Culture*. Trans. Richard Nice. London: Sage, 1977 [1970].
Bourdieu, Pierre, et al. *The Weight of the World: Social Suffering in Contemporary Society*. Trans. Priscilla Parkhurst Ferguson [*Misère du monde*]. Cambridge: Polity Press, 1999.
Bowen, John. *Can Islam Be French? Pluralism and Pragmatism in a Secularist State*. Princeton: Princeton University Press, 2010.
Bras, J.-P., S. Mervin, S. Amghar, L. Fournier, O. Marongiu, and B. Godard. «L'enseignement de l'Islam dans les écoles coraniques les institutions de formation islamique et les écoles privées.» Rapport du IISMM & EHESS, 2010. http://www.disons.fr/wp-content/uploads/2012/03/RAPPORTENSEIGNEMENT-ISLAMIQUE-final.pdf.
Chaar, Nada. «Pourquoi l'école française reproduit-elle les inégalités?» *Slate*, 24 janvier 2017. http://www.slate.fr/story/134963/pourquoi-eleves-reussissent-pas-ecole.
Durand, Anne-Aël. «Au-delà de l'emballement, l'enseignement de l'arabe reste ultraminoritaire à l'école.» *Le Monde*, 11 September 2018. https://www.lemonde.fr/les-decodeurs/article/2018/09/11/au-dela-de-l-emballement-l-enseignement-de-l-arabe-reste-ultraminoritaire-a-l-ecole_5353565_4355770.html.
Durpaire, François, et Béatrice Mabilon-Bonfils. *Fatima moins bien notée que Marianne: L'islam et l'école de la République*. La Tour d'Aigues: L'Aube, 2016.
Ferrara, Carol. "Religious Tolerance and Understanding in the French Education System." *Religious Education* 107.5 (2012): 514–530.
Ferrara, Carol. "Transmitting Faith in the Republic: Muslim Schooling in Modern Plural France." *Religious Education* 113.1 (2018): 14–25.
Gasol, Jean, André Blandin, and Pierre Tournemire. «Des témoins ont la parole II.» *L'Etat et l'enseignement privé*. Ed. Bruno Poucet. Rennes: Presses universitaires de Rennes, 2011. 65–86.
Gharrafi, Miloud. «L'enseignement de l'arabe en France: entre choix institutionnel et renvoi identitaire.» *Colloque international: Langues en immigration, mutation et nouveaux enjeux*. Rabat, Maroc, 2011. 127–131.

Ghouati, Ahmed. «Langue et communication interculturelle. Le cas de l'enseignement de la langue arabe en France.» *Langues et médias en Méditerranée: usages et réception.* Ed. A. Lachkar. Paris: l'Harmattan, 2012. 112–122.

Keaton, Trica Danielle. *Muslim Girls and the Other France: Race, Identity Politics, and Social Exclusion.* Indiana University Press, 2006.

Lorcerie, Françoise. "A French Approach to Minority Islam? A Study in Normative Confusion." *Journal of International Migration and Integration* 11.1 (February 2010): 59–72.

Lorcerie, Françoise. «Y a-t-il des élèves musulmans?» *Diversité* (168), Dossier Retour sur la question ethnique (avril 2012): 64–73.

McCormack, Jo. *Collective Memory: France and the Algerian War (1954–1962).* Lanham: Lexington Books, 2007.

Peyronie, Karima. «La langue arabe, sujet de discorde?» *Salam News* 59 (September–October 2016): 10–11.

Poucet, Bruno. *La liberté sous contrat. Une histoire de l'enseignement privé.* Paris: Fabert, 2009.

Puzenat, Amélie. *Conversions à l'islam.* Rennes: Presses Universitaires de Rennes, 2015.

Ramadan, Tariq. *Etre occidental et musulman aujourd'hui.* Paris: Presses du Châtelet, 2015.

Toulemonde, Bernard. «La naissance de «l'» enseignement privé.» *Revue française d'administration publique* 79 (juillet–septembre 1996): 445–459.

Van Bruinessen, Martin, and Stefano Allievi. *Producing Islamic Knowledge: Transmission and Dissemination in Western Europe.* London and New York: Routledge, 2011.

Zaman, Mujadad, and Nadeem A. Memon, eds. *Philosophies of Islamic Education: Historical Perspectives and Emerging Discourses.* New York: Routledge, 2016.

Conclusion

Diversity and Integration

While the schools visited for this study share many similarities in terms of motivation, implementation, and goals, other projects differ widely, despite being a part of one clear momentum. Full-time Muslim schools confirm the diversity of Muslim French that was emphasized in Chapter 1. It should be emphasized again that this diversity is within one group of the Muslim community, since there are French Muslims in France who are not at all associated with such endeavors.

The diversity of the schools is also reflected in their onomastic choices: those who purposefully look for a Muslim French with a name "indigenous" to modern France (such as converts Eva De Vitray and Philippe Grenier[1]) to those who use a name from the glorious Muslim past, be it intellectuals/scientists who are symbols of an alliance of West and East (Averroès, Al-Kindi, Ibn Khaldoun), or a place crossroads of cultures (Samarcande), to universal symbols of literacy (La Plume), some with explicit reference to the Scriptures (Iqra) or Arabic (Alif). Others simply emphasize achievement (Réussite, Excellence) and knowledge (Education et Savoir, La Lumière du Savoir), others are generic (Nouvel Horizon).[2]

We can conclude that the opening of Muslim schools is a sign of integration for three reasons. First, Muslims are claiming their share of confessional schools alongside the other major religions in France. There

© The Editor(s) (if applicable) and The Author(s) 2019
C. Bourget, *Islamic Schools in France*,
https://doi.org/10.1007/978-3-030-03834-2

cannot be a double standard, as Bowen noted in his analysis of a different situation in a slanted documentary: "ironically, the more closely Trappes Muslims imitated past generations of French social movements and political groups, the less well-integrated they are judged to be" (2007: 177). No such criticism is levied against practicing Catholics who send their children to Catholic schools, and the same can be said for Jews, though some people do voice concerns about some Jewish schools in particular. Schools from minority groups are more targeted than the majority group, and Muslim schools can expect to suffer from a double standard compared to other confessional schools for a long time, be it in France, Western Europe, or Canada (Tremblay 55).

Second, Muslims have mustered the education and the means to claim the benefits the French state has to offer to religious communities, and Muslim parents who are registering their children there have assimilated one of the long-held views of the French who resort to private schools: the quality of education first. Although some are deploring the opening of confessional schools, the religious factor is an added value, but the primary reason remains academic excellence. It is not a coincidence that schools are located in areas where the public system is widely seen as having failed.

Third, and most importantly, these schools are a sign of integration because they participate in the making of an Islam of France when they have a religious education component specifically targeted to the French context. As Jonathan Laurence states that the "process of emancipation and domestication will likely span generations, and it has only just begun" for Europe's Muslims (162), the creation of these schools is one indication that that process is well under way in France. Moreover, the religion classes participate in the development of an Islam of France, as opposed to Islam in France, by making it a priority to help students reconcile their identity as French Muslims, or Muslim French, something that is more often than not considered to be an oxymoron by Islamophobes.

In his book analyzing the discourses of prominent Muslim French intellectuals, Gemie concludes his chapter on Tariq Ramadan by contrasting Ramadan with Chahdortt Djavann and Fadela Amara, who both prone complete assimilation, by referring to Homi Bhabha's concept of a Third Space (132). According to Gemie, "Ramadan is clearly proposing something different, and perhaps his call to Muslims to enact their faith within European society is a better example of what 'Third Space' thought might look like. One lesson we can gain from Ramadan is that this is a difficult space: one can see how Ramadan's thought inhabits a strange area between the reified, ossified versions of Islam represented by groups like the Wahabis, the close-minded centralism of French Republicanism and a happy postmodern relativism, in which all cultures are equally grey. Ramadan is an ethical, emancipatory thinker: like the earlier Liberation Theologians, his overriding concern is to assist the self-emancipation of the powerless" (132). The founding of private confessional schools by Muslim French, aiming for a contract with the State, can be seen as an example of this self-liberated Third space.

CHALLENGES

Muslim schools face the same problems as all private schools. According to a teacher, one of the biggest challenges for teachers nowadays stems from the extremes of the benevolent pedagogy in which children are raised, believing that they have the right to do anything, and dealing with "intrusive families:" parents excuse their children, question and no longer respect teachers. Teachers thus end up not only educating students but also managing parents that are heavily involved in their children's education, and while this problem is everywhere, it is all the more present in private schools because parents pay tuition. I was told in a couple of schools that there is a kind of consumer behavior: families expect the school to answer certain requests because they pay to be there, this was mentioned to me as an issue in private education in general.

But these pale compared to the additional issues that stem from the fact that they are Muslim private schools. As we have seen, Muslim schools face increasing challenges regarding their financing (as contracts are not systematically attributed after five years even when conditions are met), their opening (the 2018 Gatel law has made it harder), and one opposition in the bureaucratic wheel is all it takes to sink a project. I was told in 2018 that there were only 11 additional classes funded last year to Muslim schools. In addition, one school board member was much worried about the development of the network Ecoles Espérance-banlieues, which have been set up in areas with a high percentage of Muslims. Grégory Chambat has shown that this movement is associated with a Catholic Far right with a "colonial attitude" (Ranc) in order to slow down the development of Muslim schools.

While browsing the web for information about IFSQY, I came across a piece of information that shows some of the ignorance and attitudes that Muslim schools face. The minutes of a cycling club include a letter from one of Samarcande's teachers who is asking if a member of the club can come as a guest speaker to her fifth-grade class in the context of a unit about sharing the road. What the minutes reflect are not a discussion about the feasibility of the request, but some information gathered about the school: that it is a "private Muslim school," that it is named after a "city in Uzbekistan," that the request for a contract with the state was denied in 2014, that "wearing a headscarf is authorized, contrary to French law" and that it offers Muslim religion classes.[3] These details and how they are phrased and presented contribute to Othering the school (named after a foreign city), situating its practices outside of French law (wrongfully so since the ban on religious signs does not apply to private schools). Even the mention that its request for a contract with the State was denied implies that the school must have done something wrong since it is presented as a negative without being fully informed of the process and reasons for denial. Given this framing, it is not surprising that eleven out of sixteen members voted to turn down the request.

In addition, even people who can be sympathetic have reservations about Muslim schools, some from a principle point of being staunch defenders and supporters of a unified public school system. Even writers who seem to be more open-minded and aware of the increased prejudice faced by these schools are not immune. For instance, Patrick Tapernoux points out the misguided attitude of many teachers in the public system who refuse to give some recognition to the Muslim backgrounds of some of their students, whether they justify it on the grounds of secularism, democratic values, centralism, or an already overloaded curriculum (154). He is also critical of the way secularism is being implemented in France and advocates for making room for religions in schools and not preventing religious practices (157). But he himself refers to Muslim schools as Qur'anic schools ("écoles coraniques" 13), showing that he does not understand the difference between a weekend school where the focus is on Islam's Holy book and full-time Muslim schools that teach the national curriculum. He also talks about girls wearing a tchador (184), which is a full-body covering cloth, instead of the scarf worn by some girls. Furthermore, he raises suspicion about associations that organize after-school tutoring, stating that often, Islamic fundamentalists hide behind them, but does not cite any names.[4]

One former non-Muslim teacher who worked a few years at Averroès might be representative of many with strong reservations about Muslim schools. While he was categorical about the fact that Zitouni's statements were false and defamatory, he felt ambivalent toward projects such as Averroès. On the one hand, he made great friendships, was full of praise for one of the religion teachers whom he described as very intelligent and open, and praised the administration who gave him carte blanche. But he was critical about several points: foreign financing when the school expansion was financed by a Qatari charity,[5] invitation of Tareq Oubrou, an imam, in the context of a civics and moral class; lack of critical distance from teachers from the pressure of their community, particularly when it comes to a discourse of victimization; the fact that he saw former students having difficulty integrating the larger society after leaving Averroès. He also thought that the goal of the school was really to form an elite who would then push for their "caprices communautaires" "communautarian whims." When I asked him to elaborate what he meant by that, he mentioned the "revendications politiques permanentes" "permanent political claims" such as wearing the scarf. He also added that he was against Jewish schools as well because they reinforce *communautarisme*, but not against Catholic schools (with which he also has experience) because they have a mix of people. His reaction about the scarf can be paralleled to one of the three categories[6] listed in Bowen's (2007) study, that is, "acts that offend only within the specific logic of laïcité in the French school (such as breaking the Ramadan fast on school grounds)" (163). This particular understanding of laïcité is a perfect example of the double standard Islam is subjected to: having fish in school cafeterias on Friday is not seen equivalent to halal meat or eating at a different time than lunch even though they all have at their origin a religious practice.

The concern about students being able to integrate into larger society is a pointed one, and one that some schools are acutely aware of and address in different ways. Eva de Vitray, for instance, will stop at middle school for that very reason. All directors I spoke with hope to have a more diversified student population in the future, not just because it would be a proof of success that their academic reputation would prompt more non-Muslim parents to enroll their children. Averroès' students have discussions to prepare them about that issue. In one class I visited, at some point, a student recalled a discussion they had in class the year before that had concluded that they shouldn't be only "entre-soi" otherwise they will be lost when they go to college in a different environment. Indeed, some former students from Averroès and Al Kindi experienced difficulty making the transition between their small-knit Muslim school and university. One student told Ferrara that "it was her first real experience with judgment and criticism from her co-citizens since in many respects she was shielded from this at Averroès" (Ferrara 2018: 19). But the majority of students she interviewed claimed the opposite: that being in a Muslim school gave them confidence that helped them to reach out to new friends, answer critical questions from curious people, and perhaps more importantly, "many students specifically acknowledged the strong discourse of French Muslim identity making that helped them to understand how to bridge the gap between "being Muslim" and "being French"" (Ferrara 2018: 21).

One religion teacher was very optimistic about the future of Islam in France, partially—and paradoxically—thanks to books such as Houellebeq's *Soumission*, which, even though it is Islamophobic, is a sign of the tensions that inevitably come during a period of transition. According to him, there is a Renaissance of Islam in the West and in France in particular, but people need to realize that Islam is not engaged in a political project.

Future Challenges: Gender and Federations

Gender

While SMIC is an acronym for minimum wage, Bajrafil, a young imam from Vitry-sur-Seine used the phrase "smic de la foi" and redefined SMIC as standing for "le savoir minimum indispensable à une conversation" "the minimum knowledge required for a conversation" on faith. According to him, politicians in France should have a minimum understanding of the faith of their few million Muslim fellow citizens (cited by Darnault). One sticky point that remains regarding anything related to Islam in France is linked to gender and the widespread conviction that Islam oppresses women.

From cities to villages, engravings in the facade of many public buildings remind us that there were schools for girls ("écoles de filles") and schools for boys ("écoles de garçons") as recently as fifty years ago. Co-ed classrooms are a relatively new development in France; it started in 1962 and was generalized by a memo in June 1969 (Duval 37).

CONCLUSION 159

Despite debates of researchers about the pros and cons of co-education, it is taken for granted as a progress toward gender equality in France.[7] This also helps explain why gender is always a concern in schools, and Islam has in part served as a scapegoat and a convenient blinker to gender issues that are still very much present in French culture at large.

Entrance of a former girls' school, Grenoble, September 2016

In his analysis of the press coverage of the controversy over the opening of Al Kindi and the strong opposition it faced, Mazawi shows that there is always a specification as to whether women and girls are veiled or not. He concludes that "The manifestation and regulation of women's/girls' bodies in public schools *versus* Muslim schools are instituted as mutually exclusive *embodied* dichotomies. At the same time, Muslim boys remain textually absent. Men are represented as fathers, activists or association officials (and one as teacher) while activist women are passivated or conspicuously absent. Al Kindi can thus be implicitly labelled as 'modernist', 'conservative' or 'traditional' - without these terms being deployed in the text. I argue that it is through these intersecting binaries of absence/presence, of women/men and girls/boys, and their interplays, that the identities of Muslims are racialised and locked 'into fixed species of otherness'" (251–252).

I paid attention to gender dynamics in the schools, and noted the proportion of girls wearing a headscarf in the classes I visited. The percentage of veiled girls in all elementary classes I observed was 0%. While I was in the elementary school at al Kindi, classes were interrupted by a fire drill, so I got to see all elementary school students at once in the playground neatly standing in rows; I counted 2 veiled girls (out of more than a hundred students). For middle school grades, the averages per school were 30, 39, 44, and 60% (again for the middle school classes I sat in). For high school grades, the average percentages were 47, 86, and 100%. To counter assumptions some readers might draw, I will specify that the class where 100% of girls were veiled was at MHS, the only school that does not offer religion classes (but there were non-veiled girls in that school as well). Though my sample might not be statistically sound, it seems logical that the percentages increase with age, plus one needs to remember that the veiled girls would be barred from public schools. I did not see any gender segregation in the schools I visited, with the exception of an announcement for a workshop for girls only on promiscuity, and separate lunch rooms in another. Seating arrangements were mixed, maybe with a higher tendency for girls to sit next to girls in the higher grades, but not always, which might be seen in any school. In one school, I saw boys and girls engaged in a spontaneous and intense soccer game with mixed teams during a break.

In the course of several conversations with a teacher in her thirties, she made it clear to me that based on her experience and her peers', there has been a hardening of anti-Islam positions in France that are making the situation more and more difficult, particularly for women who chose to wear a headscarf. Self-described as a French woman of parents who were themselves brought to France at a young age, she was not religious at all, nor was her family, but mainstream society kept reminding her that she was not really French by asking about her origins. Answering the question "where are you from" with the area of France where she was born invariably triggered a follow-up (but really, originally), the implication being that someone with an Arabic name cannot really be just from metropolitan France. At age 19, because of being constantly reminded of her origins not by her family, but by society at large, she began to learn about these origins. She started praying, which freaked her parents out. They did not give her a religious education, and her decision to start wearing a scarf was not welcomed by her family who summoned her to try to understand what was wrong with her. She herself has two children in a Muslim school, and her main motivation to have them there is not the Arabic and the Qur'an, which they could learn with a tutor or at the weekend school, but to make sure that they can live their identity peacefully, without being discriminated against.

While the 2004 law banned religious signs from public schools only, it paved the way for discrimination in other settings. There are many incidents of women being fired from their jobs, most notably the Baby Loup case.[8] Even though the law does not apply to private schools, one teacher I spoke with applied to teach in Catholic schools, had an interview over the phone, then in person was told that her headscarf did not respect the principle of secularism so therefore she could not be hired because they were under contract with the State. Several teachers I spoke with had been clearly emotionally hurt at different times by the hostility they encountered, one in particular when she was asked to show her ears before taking the entrance exam for medical school, not because she was asked to show her ears but because of the demeaning manner in which it was done. A recent article and video about MHS students being overly searched while talking the Bac exam in another high school show that women are the most susceptible to this kind of harassment.

Many female teachers in the schools I visited were veiled, including most primary school teachers at two different locations, though with different styles (headscarf, abayas, head turbans that showed the neck). As was already noted by the 2010 report, veiled women are barred from public service, so Muslim schools are one of the few places where women can work and be free to wear the headscarf (Bras et al. 48).

The 2004 law affects some Muslim schools' staff when they have to go for training, usually in other schools, as I was told by a History and Geography teacher who wears a headscarf. Because some of the classes she teaches are under contract with the State, she is required to attend training days that are organized by the Ministry of education, and on a couple of occasions, she was prevented from attending because of her headscarf. She knows of similar incidents, and says it is really up to the good will of the principal of the school that happens to be hosting the training session. Such incidents echo what happened throughout the 15 years that the controversy over the headscarf worn by pupils in public schools lasted: a case-by-case approach. As more and more Muslim schools' classes get contracts, this problem will intensify.

Federations

The decentralization law in 1985, which, among other things, delegated the financing of some of the operation expenses for secondary schools to local authorities, pushed private Catholic schools into organizing themselves to have representatives at the level of the region and the Academy (Toulemonde, "Naissance" 448). Given that Catholic and Jewish schools have federations to represent them, it was only a matter of time until Muslim schools would also create a federation to represent them. There are three groupings so far of Muslim schools, a fact that reflects their lack of unity: those who joined the FNEM, those who joined the UEPM, and those who have not (yet) or refused to join either.

FNEM

The Fédération Nationale de l'Enseignement privé Musulman (FNEM) was the first federation of Muslim schools, created in March 2014 as an initiative by five schools to defend their interests and be their interlocutor and representative with the Ministry of Education. On its website, it lists the schools it labels as "pioneers" and their founding dates as follows: La Plume (2001), Averroès (2003), Al-Kindi (2007), Education et savoir (2008), and Ibn Khaldoun (2009). Makhlouf Mamècheis president of the FNEM, which is at the same time its strength and its weakness. He is also one of the assistant principals of Averroès, and most importantly, vice-president of the UOIF. His membership with the UOIF, which is widely considered as a branch of the Muslim Brothers, is the reason several schools gave me for not joining the FNEM. Indeed, four of the five pioneers have ties with the UOIF, usually through their founders' affiliation.

While the report published in 2010 noted that the increase in the number of schools was in part due to the militancy of the Muslim Brothers in the perspective of promoting a Muslim citizenship, my discussions and observations lead me to see the UOIF as taking over rather than initiating some of the projects that are attributed to it. The FNEM acknowledges on its website that it is not the catalyst behind the movement to open Muslim schools, and that the creation of Muslim schools is a reaction to a demand from families. Its founding members are constantly solicited for advice by people who would like to open schools, therefore by founding the FNEM, they simply answered a "demonstrated schooling need" "besoin scolaire reconnu."[9]

In 2015, the FNEM organized a conference inviting the directors of their Catholic, Protestant, and Jewish homologues, as well as staff from the Ministry of Education such as inspector Bernard Toulemonde. In his introductory speech, Mamèche states that Muslim schools' strength and success will be to "reconcile the République's and Islam's values." That year, Mamèche mentions a total of 38 Muslim schools in France plus about 50 projects.[10]

Obviously, the directors of Averroès and Al Kindi support the FNEM. Averroes' principal thinks that it will help new schools projects to avoid mistakes, and will provide a needed guidance because many are started by people who do not have any educational background, and that children's education is at stake. The FNEM would provide a minimum of organization and facilitate the process, and also avoid that schools be used as pawns by various political parties. He went on to mention Algeria, Morocco, Turkey, and the UOIF. When I pointed out the close association between the UOIF and the FNEM, he said that Averroes, Al Kindi, and Ibn Khaldoun are under the umbrella of the UOIF, but disputed the close ties to the Muslim Brothers that the UOIF is always accused of. He said that one can be influenced by the writings and thought of the Muslim Brotherhood without belonging to the movement. The UOIF advocates an Islam of France, and many Muslims in France are living a balanced Islam (Interview September 2016). The assistant principal added that the FNEM simply functions as equivalent to the Secrétariat général Catholique, that is a direct interlocutor to the Ministry.

When I interviewed Mamèche in 2016, he added that one goal of the FNEM is to establish a curriculum for ethics classes, to ensure the future of teaching Islam in schools. He considers the fact that he was invited in a meeting organized by the Ministry with inspectors on May 31, 2016 as a sign of recognition. There were about 60 Muslim schools in France when we spoke in 2016, and he projected that in the next five years, there could be a total of 200. But only 7 Muslim schools were under contract with the state: Al Kindi alone counted for 3 (primary, junior high, and high school), the others were Averroes, Ibn Khaldoun, and IFSQY. He also pointed out that in many cases, only one or two classes are under contract. Averroes was lucky to get all its high school classes under contract at once, it seems that most recently the policy has been to allocate funding one class at a time, and schools must renew their request every year.

The FNEM believes that a contract is the best way for the State to oversee and control what is going on in schools, not only because of the financial support but also the pedagogical one. The FNEM accepts all schools as members, even those who do not want a contract (though he points out that most of these are ill-informed that they would lose their specific character, but others want to keep their complete independence). According to him, most of the new schools are primary schools for two reasons: it is much easier and cheaper to start an elementary school than a secondary school, and many families think that it is important to give a strong foundation to children from the start because once they reach secondary school, it is too late.

UEPM

Another federation was created in 2016, the Union Européenne pour l'Enseignement privé Musulman (UEPM), widely referred to when I inquired about it to some of the schools I visited in 2018 as "the Turkish" federation.[11] According to its website, it was founded in 2016 and aims to create a network of French and European schools, which is an added dimension compared to the FNEM.[12] Indeed, its annual congress took place during the annual conference organized by Milli Görüs on April 29, 2018. A summary on the website lists the report delivered during the conference, which states that there are eight operating member schools, two that will open in Fall 2018, and five in preparation.[13] Its four founding member schools are:

- Groupe Scolaire Bellevue Muhammed Hamidullah (preK-9) in Clichy sous Bois (Paris region)
- Groupe Scolaire La Lumière du Savoir (preK-6) in Corbeil-Essonnes (Paris region)
- Collège Eyyub Sultan in Strasbourg (6-9) (Alsace)
- La Maison d'Arqam (1-5) in Vénissieux (Lyon region)

The UEPM's objectives are similar to the FNEM's: help existing schools and projects, be a representative instance, and facilitate collaboration and activities among schools. As an effort of coordination, the UEPM launched a petition against the Gatel law discussed in Chapter 2.

I got in touch with Bellevue school, which is the Headquarter for the UEPM, hoping to visit and/or interview the director. I had spoken to a secretary and decided to try my luck and show up. I had a conversation with a parent who had come to pick up a sick child while she was waiting for her daughter to be brought out. When the director (related to the founder of the UEPM) escorted the child out, I finally got the chance to address her directly, but she wouldn't talk to me because she was too busy.

Independent

While the 2010 report notes an opposition between the UOIF, engaged in a national and European strategy, and those in strong relations with countries of origin of immigrants and their descendants (Bras et al. 75), there is another group of schools that refuse to be associated with any such group and remain independent. According to schools that have refused to join either the FNEM or the UEPM, having federations that are aligned with a specific ideology is a mistake because it fragments by integrating a cultural dimension or a religious movement.

Indeed, the main reproach to the FNEM in particular is its affiliation with an ideological movement, and especially one that is targeted by politicians. Schools fear that they will be labeled UOIF by joining the FNEM. Other recurring objections to the FNEM were the absence of consultation and participation, and lack of a pedagogical project.[14] Also schools do not want imposition from higher up, and some schools resent that the FNEM speaks in their names without their authorization. One person was particularly critical of Lasfar who promoted Averroes to the detriment of other schools. Bowen noted the contrast between the Islamic council that is "part of national politics" and the Islamic associations who are "strongly anchored in cities or even neighborhoods, and enter only warily and provisionally into large-scale federations" (48–49). This seems to be playing out also with schools.

Nevertheless, these schools recognize the need for a Muslim network independent of any movement that can be an interlocutor, and that in the long term, schools can't continue operating without consulting and coordinating with one another. One school remarked that another Muslim school had opened nearby, but they do not have any relationship with them. One school was considering establishing a federation at the level of the Academy that administers their area. According to one director, a federation will not work because there are too many divisions, competition, and enviousness. Another person told me that the founders of Fort School were parents of children in La Réussite who led a coup in 2014 to throw out the school board and take it over. The coup failed, and they opened Fort School.[15] If anything, these disagreements, to put it mildly, show the heterogeneity of approaches to Muslim schools projects, and that while there are instances of cooperation between schools, there are also internecine fights and disagreements that can sabotage a project.

Paradoxically, we see that the efforts to federate Muslim schools reflect their division and lack of unity. While there has been a clear impetus for opening more schools, and while some federations like the FNEM are clearly trying to bring them together, one cannot speak of a monolithic, unified movement by the Muslim community, despite the many similarities one can hear from school to school regarding the motivations in particular.

Conclusion

As I write these final lines in the post-World cup victory euphoria in July 2018, parallels are both made and rejected with the "Black Blanc Beur" victory of 1998, when France won its first World Cup, thanks to a multicultural team, with race and ethnicity being the markers of focus. Twenty years later, Islam has become a legitimate topic on the football field, with concerns expressed about the Muslim players on the team handling fasting during the month of Ramadan with the training to prepare for the tournament, and emphasizing that the seven Muslims[16] out of 23 players on the team were given the freedom to make their own decisions and have chosen not to fast.[17] Two years before, during the Euro Tournament, Didier Deschamps, the coach of the French team, dismissed any questions linked to previous controversies about offering halal buffets by stating that they wanted players to "feel at ease".[18] Before the 2018 World Cup, the issue is raised again in the press, and Deschamps is quoted as saying that there is neither "issue nor debate", that the players are free to make their decision and that the staff will plan accordingly because they want to "put them in the best conditions" (Delom). Let's hope that the lessons from 1998 have been learned, and that the euphoria of this second victory and the benevolence granted to the Muslim players regarding Islam will yield to more openness not only for the soccer star team, comprised of about one quarter to one-third Muslims, but to all Muslim French.

Notes

1. The first Muslim representative in the Parliament at the turn of the twentieth century http://www.unicite38.fr/index.php?option=com_chronoforms5&view=form&Itemid=246.
2. Virtually all students in all classes I visited had Arabic names (or names common to both such as Sarah). One parent in a school thinks that parents should start naming their children with French names to make it easier for them. Pointing out the example of a little girl in the school, Marie, daughter of a "Franco-French" family who converted to Islam, she noted that Marie with her "unmarked" first name and last name, even though she is Muslim, will most likely face much less discrimination than someone whose name would be easily identified as Muslim. She knows of an Arab Muslim family who named a son Noé instead of the Arabic version. When I asked her, taking a motto I had heard from someone else (one should integrate without disintegrating), whether it was a disintegration, she reminded me that her generation was essentially of French culture, therefore the answer to my question was a resounding no.
3. « 2.1 Demande de formation reçue le 31/10 Message reçu: Je suis professeure des écoles de la classe de CM2 de l'école Samarcande (IFSQY) à Montigny le Bretonneux, et je dois faire passer l'Attestation de Première Éducation à la Route à mes élèves cette année. Pour ce faire, nous devons travailler sur l'usage de l'espace routier en tant rouleur avec différentes pratiques en classe, à l'école ou à l'extérieur de l'école. Afin de fournir la meilleure formation à nos élèves, je souhaite savoir s'il est envisageable d'obtenir l'intervention d'un membre de votre association qui pourra apporter un regard professionnel sur le cyclisme. Compte-rendu réunion bureau VCMB Cyclo du 14 novembre 2017 Page 6 Cette action se fera durant la dernière période scolaire c'est à dire entre le 4 juin 2018 et le 4 juillet 2018. Dans l'attente de votre retour, je vous prie de croire, Madame, Monsieur, à l'expression de ma considération distinguée. Mme ASRI. L'IFSQY est un institut de formation, « une école privée musulmane », située: 3 Rue François Geoffre, 78180 Montigny-le-Bretonneux, France; ancien locaux des impôts... site internet: www.ifsqy.fr Le groupe scolaire privé de l'Institut devient Collège /Lycée Samarcande (ville d'Ouzbékistan). Etablissement privé hors contrat avec l'éducation

nationale demande refusé en 2014. Le port du voile est accepté, contrairement à la loi française. Des cours de religion musulmane sont dispensés. Question aux membres du comité directeur: La section cyclo répond-elle positivement à cette demande? Oui: 3 voies; Abstention: 2 voies; Non: 11 voies. Une réponse sera faite par le président que nous ne pouvons pas répondre positivement à ce besoin.»https://www.vcmb.fr/cyclo/phocadownload/VCMB/bureau_cr_reunion/vcmb_cr_reunion_2017-11-14.pdf.

4. « Une enquête que nous menons actuellement dans des banlieues dites « difficiles » nous prouve que, derrière le travail des associations d'aide aux devoirs des enfants migrants, se cachent souvent des officines de propagande d'intégristes islamiques qui font, au demeurant, un excellent travail à l'aune des résultats scolaires! » I could not locate any publication from him that would give the results of his enquiry.
5. He used a strong phrase connoting physical violence to say that "j'ai été agressé par le financement étranger," literally "I was assaulted by the foreign financing."
6. The other two were "clearly offensive acts" and "acts that might attest to sheer ignorance" (163).
7. See, for instance, Nicole Mosconi.
8. https://www.lemonde.fr/societe/article/2013/11/27/l-affaire-baby-loup-en-quatre-questions_3520954_3224.html.
9. http://www.fnem.fr/business-01/#4.
10. http://www.fnem.fr/premieres-assises-nationales-de-lenseignement-musulman-discours-de-makhlouf-mameche/.
11. The potential "Turkish" connection is only evident for three out of the four schools, either because of Turkish offered as a foreign language (Maison d'Arqam, Eyyûb Sultan), the Turkish origin of the directors (Bellevue), or the name of the school (Eyyûb Sultan).
12. http://www.ueepm.fr/.
13. http://www.ueepm.fr/communique-de-luepm-suite-au-congres-de-la-cimg-france-le-29-avril-2018/.
14. One school that was a founding member said that the FNEM got more out of having them join than the other way around. Being a member did not bring anything to the school, but the FNEM was able to showcase a woman.
15. I was supposed to interview the director of Fort School, but he bailed out on me at the last minute.
16. The actual number of Muslim players is up for debate but is probably closer to eight. In one article, 6 players were explicitly listed as Muslims, but did not pretend that the list was exhaustive (Farelli).

17. https://www.lequipe.fr/Football/Article/Equipe-de-france-ramadan-et-amenagements/903640, http://www.leparisien.fr/sports/football/coupe-du-monde/mondial-2018-comment-les-joueurs-musulmans-gerent-le-ramadan-05-06-2018-7754607.php, http://sport.le360.ma/football/equipe-de-france-deschamps-fixe-la-regle-pour-le-ramadan-57275.
18. http://www.lepoint.fr/sport/football/euro-2016/euro-2016-equipe-de-france-comment-les-bleus-vivent-leur-foi-12-06-2016-2046084_3061.php.

References

Bras, J.-P., S. Mervin, S. Amghar, L. Fournier, O. Marongiu, and B. Godard. "L'enseignement de l'Islam dans les écoles coraniques les institutions de formation islamique et les écoles privées." Rapport du IISMM & EHESS, 2010. http://www.disons.fr/wp-content/uploads/2012/03/RAPPORTENSEIGNEMENT-ISLAMIQUE-final.pdf.
Bowen, John. *Why the French Don't Like Headscarves: Islam, the State and Public Space*. Princeton, NJ: Princeton University Press, 2007.
Darnault, Maïté. « Mohamed Bajrafil: "L'islam est par essence laïque". » *Le Monde des Religions*, 29 October 2015. http://www.lemondedesreligions.fr/actualite/mohamed-bajrafil-l-islam-est-par-essence-laique-29-10-2015-5018_118.php.
Delom, Hugo. "Ramadan et aménagements." *L'Equipe*, 23 May 2018, 4.
Duval, Nathalie. *Enseignement et education en France du XVIIIe siècle à nos jours*. Paris: Armand Colin, 2011.
Farelli, Lina. « L'équipe de France, reflet d'une diversité qui gagne et qui doit gagner toutes les sphères. » *SaphirNews*, 16 Juillet 2018. https://www.saphirnews.com/L-equipe-de-France-reflet-d-une-diversite-qui-gagne-et-qui-doit-gagner-toutes-les-spheres_a25414.html.
Ferrara, Carol. "Transmitting Faith in the Republic: Muslim Schooling in Modern Plural France." *Religious Education* 113.1 (2018): 14–25.
Gemie, Sharif. *French Muslims: New Voices in Contemporary France*. Cardiff: University of Wales Press, 2010.
Laurence, Jonathan. *The Emancipation of Europe's Muslims: The State's Role in Minority Integration*. Princeton: Princeton University Press, 2011.
Mazawi, André. « Qui a peur du lycée musulman? » "Media Representations of a Muslim School in France." *Social Semiotics* 19.3 (September 2009): 235–256.
Mosconi, Nicole. « Effets et limites de la mixité scolaire. » *Travail, genre et sociétés* 11.1 (2004): 165–174.

Ranc, Agathe. « Innovantes ou réac? 5 questions sur les écoles Espérance banlieues. » *L'Obs*, 19 mars 2017. https://www.nouvelobs.com/education/20170315.OBS6637/innovantes-ou-reac-5-questions-sur-les-ecoles-esperance-banlieues.html.

Tapernoux, Patrick. *Les enseignants du « privé ». Tribu catholique?* Paris: Anthropos, 2001.

Toulemonde, Bernard. « La naissance de « l' » enseignement privé. » *Revue française d'administration publique* 79 (juillet–septembre 1996): 445–459.

Tremblay, Stéphanie. « Religion, « communauté » et citoyenneté: le cas des écoles Steiner, musulmane et juive en contexte montréalais. » *Diversité urbaine* 12.2 (2012): 53–68.

Index

A
Academic failure, 29, 30, 80, 88, 125
Al Kindi, xix–xxi, 15, 64–68, 70, 72, 158, 159, 163
Allah, 135, 138, 140, 142, 145, 147.
 See also God
Alternative meal, 14, 127
Amana, 119
APCS, 117–119
Arab, 3, 6, 9, 67, 97, 106, 115, 133, 135, 149, 167
Arabic, xix, xxi, xxii, 55–57, 59, 62, 63, 70, 76–78, 80, 87, 92, 93, 100–102, 105, 108, 111, 112, 117, 121, 127, 132–138, 140, 141, 143, 147–149, 153, 160, 161, 167
Assimilation, xvi, xviii, 9, 11, 14, 94, 154
Averroès, 15, 56–61, 72, 117, 120, 122, 157, 158, 162, 163

B
Banlieues/suburb, 55, 66, 76, 88, 106, 108, 116, 155

Beur, 3, 166
Billon, Annick, 99
Bourdieu, Pierre, 125, 126, 149
Bowen, John, xvi, 5, 14–16, 76, 77, 82, 84, 129, 132, 149, 154, 157
Bras, J.-P., xv, 57, 58, 63, 64, 70, 118, 132, 138, 161, 165
Budget, 23, 29, 30, 43, 58, 60, 68, 79, 83, 84, 90, 101, 109, 115

C
Caractère proper/specific character, 13, 23, 25, 28, 57, 164
Catholicism, 12, 41
 Catholic Church, 19–21, 33, 42, 66
 Catholic schools, 13, 19–22, 27, 32, 35, 38, 39, 41, 59, 88, 91, 154, 157, 161, 162
Césari, Jocelyne, 3, 7
Co-ed, 36, 58, 129, 149, 158
Cohen, Erik, 13, 34–36, 38, 39
Colonial, xiii, xiv, 9, 130
Communautarisme, xvi, xviii, 4–7, 11, 13, 14, 66, 133, 157

172 INDEX

Community, xiii, xvi, 4, 5, 7, 8, 21,
    31, 34, 35, 39, 60, 77, 88, 105,
    109, 111, 113, 142, 153, 157,
    166
Concordat, 12, 21, 28
Contract, xviii–xx, 22–25, 27, 30–32,
    38–40, 42, 57–59, 61, 68, 72,
    75, 82–87, 90, 91, 94, 96, 99,
    101, 106, 109–111, 115, 119,
    120, 122, 134, 155, 156, 161,
    163, 164. *See also* Subsidies
Cultural capital, 126
Cultural heritage, 44, 126
Curriculum, xv, xviii, xxi, 23, 24, 31,
    34, 39, 40, 56, 62, 63, 67, 76,
    78, 80, 89, 100, 102, 103, 108,
    114, 119, 129, 130, 138, 144,
    149, 156
  national, xiii–xv, 5, 7, 8, 11, 20–24,
    26, 28, 31, 41, 43, 45, 56, 59,
    60, 67, 77, 78, 80, 83, 84, 86,
    88–90, 100, 103, 108, 110,
    117, 120, 128, 129, 133, 134,
    139, 148, 156, 165

D
Debré law, xviii, 14, 21–25, 29, 32,
    38, 40, 41
Discrimination, xviii, 9–11, 27, 40,
    131, 161, 167
Diversity, xviii, 7, 8, 13, 14, 21, 22,
    24, 43, 78, 109, 131, 148, 153
Double talk, xviii, 15, 16, 61
Durpaire, François, 129, 131

E
Education, xv, 18, 19, 21, 21, 22, 26,
    33–36, 39, 40, 43, 55, 59, 63,
    68, 100, 105, 106, 110, 114,
    118, 125, 130, 138, 140, 153,
    155, 163. *See also* School

  private, xvi, 18–22, 25, 28–30, 42,
    44, 99, 134, 155
  public, 14, 19, 20, 22, 24, 41, 105
  religious, xix, 25, 26, 39, 40, 69,
    78, 82, 88, 93, 103, 139, 154,
    161
  secular, 20
Elmaleh, Raphaël, 5, 33–40
Ethics, 56–58, 61–64, 67, 71, 72, 82,
    111, 112, 114, 115, 149, 163
Ethnic
  separatism, xv, xvi, 5
Eva de Vitray, xix, 105, 106, 108–111,
    122, 153, 157
Exclusion, xxi, 10, 55, 127, 130

F
Federation, 15, 31, 162, 164–166
Fédération Nationale de l'Enseigne-
    ment privé Musulman (FNEM),
    30, 31, 55, 135, 139, 162–166,
    168
Fernando, Mayanthi, 3, 9, 10, 12, 13
Ferrara, Carol, xxi, 61, 62, 128, 131,
    140, 158
Fredette, Jennifer, 4, 7–9, 12, 91
Funding
  public, xviii, 20

G
Gemie, Sharif, 4, 5, 15, 16, 154
Gender, xiv, xxi, 36, 40, 158–160
God, 64, 132, 140, 142–145, 147,
    148. *See also* Allah

H
Halal, xviii, 14, 57, 63, 71, 93, 109,
    145, 147, 148, 157, 166
Haram, 63, 71, 93, 109, 112,
    145–148

INDEX 173

Headscarf, xiv, xv, xviii, 4, 6, 11, 14, 78, 79, 91, 109, 112, 115, 117, 119, 127–129, 132, 156, 160, 161. *See also* Veil
affair, xiv, xv, xviii, 4, 6, 11, 14, 128, 129
Homeschooling, xx, 120
Hors contrat/non-contracted, 24, 120

I
Immigration, xiv, 11, 34, 44, 58, 133
Inequality/inequalities, 4, 126, 130
Institut de Formation de Saint-Quentin-en-Yvelines (IFSQY), xix, xx, 87, 90, 156, 163. *See also* Samarcande
Integration/intégration, xv, xvi, xviii, xxi, 4, 6, 9, 10, 13, 34, 35, 39, 153, 154. *See also* Assimilation
Interior Ministry, xv
Islam, xv–xviii, xxi, 3, 5, 7, 10, 12, 13, 13, 14, 14, 15, 27, 44, 57, 59, 61–64, 71, 78, 82, 87, 90, 93, 95, 96, 103, 106, 109, 114, 117, 121, 126, 128, 129, 131, 138–141, 144, 146, 147, 154, 155, 157–159, 163, 166
Islamic, 165. *See also* Muslim
culture, 71
schools, xv–xvii, 27
studies, xxi, 132
Islamism, xiv
Islamophobia, 10, 92, 126, 127, 139

K
Keaton, Trica, 6, 9, 125, 127–130, 148

L
Laïcité, 12, 15, 41, 157

Langouët, Gabriel, 21, 22, 28, 29, 43
La Plume, xix, xx, 75, 99–102, 122, 153, 162
La Réussite, xvi, 118, 120, 166
Lasfar, Amar, 15, 60, 61, 165
Laurence, Jonathan, 3, 4, 7, 9, 10, 12, 118, 154
Law
1905, xviii, 20, 28
2004, xiv, xv, 7, 161
Gatel, 155, 165
Local, 6, 8, 28, 32, 38, 55, 65, 66, 72, 75, 78, 84, 88, 90, 105, 106, 111, 134
administration, 22, 24, 110
authorities, 11, 13, 23, 24, 32, 58, 90, 162

M
Madrassa, 103
Makhlouf Mamèche, 31, 55, 58, 162
Media, 6–9, 14, 14, 15, 22, 42, 59, 64, 66, 86, 87, 109, 121, 139
Meskine, Dhaou, xvi, 75–77, 79, 80, 82–87, 97
Ministry of education/National education, xxii, 16, 26, 29, 31, 32, 43, 58, 60, 62, 66, 80, 84–86, 89, 97, 99, 105, 118, 128, 131, 133–135, 161–163
Morvan, Alain, 64–66
Mosque, 4, 10, 12, 13, 15, 55, 71, 82, 84, 86, 87, 93, 100, 105, 109, 115, 120, 132, 134, 136, 147
Motivation, xiii, 27–29, 35, 37, 68, 79, 88, 91, 110, 116, 132, 153, 161, 166
Muslim, 167. *See also* Islamic
Brothers, xv, 162, 163
citizen/citizenship, xiii, xv, 3, 7, 15, 103, 158, 162
education, xiii, xv, 31, 92, 93, 140

174 INDEX

French, xv, xix, xxi, 3, 7–10, 12, 15, 57, 131, 153–155, 158, 167
Muslim ethics (MHS), xix, xx, 112–117, 121, 160, 161

N
Nation, xiii–xv, xviii, 4, 28, 142
National Front, xiv
Noiriel, Gérard, 5, 11
Non-contracted, 24, 27, 99

P
Postcolonial, 9, 10
Poucet, Bruno, 13, 19–28, 32, 39–42, 44, 45, 49–51, 133, 133
Prophet, 61, 69, 95, 97, 112, 116, 138–140, 142, 144, 145, 147

Q
Qur'an, 69, 71, 76, 78, 82, 94, 96, 100, 103, 132, 135, 139–148, 161

R
Racial, 6
Racism, 6, 7, 10, 95
Radicalization, 31, 86, 129
Ramadan, Tareq, 14–16, 59, 64, 83, 116, 126, 127, 138, 139, 144, 147, 154, 155, 157, 166
Religion, xiv, xvi, xxii, 3, 4, 8, 9, 11–14, 28, 34, 35, 41, 44, 45, 55, 62, 63, 69, 71, 77, 79, 82, 87, 88, 91, 93, 96, 97, 101, 103, 110, 113, 121, 128, 129, 131, 132, 135, 137–139, 141, 149, 154, 156, 157, 160, 168
Religious signs, xiv, xv, 113, 115, 156, 161

Republic/Republican, xv, xvi, 4, 9, 12, 18–20, 66, 67, 76, 78, 108, 117, 130
Roy, Olivier, 7, 15

S
Salafi, xx, 117, 118
Samarcande, xix, xx, 87–93, 139, 156. *See also* Institut de Formation de Saint-Quentin-en-Yvelines (IFSQY)
Sarkozy, Nicolas, 15, 66, 82, 83, 87
School, 166. *See also* Education
  Catholic, 13, 19–22, 27, 32, 35, 38, 39, 41, 59, 88, 91, 110, 154, 157, 161, 162
  confessional, 14, 29, 57, 112, 153–155
  Jewish, xvi, 5, 13, 14, 19–21, 27, 32–41, 77, 86, 154, 157, 162
  Muslim/Islamic, xiii, xvi, xvii, 11, 13, 15, 15, 16, 19–22, 27, 29, 31, 32, 37, 41, 44, 56, 62, 63, 66, 72, 75–77, 86–88, 90, 99, 101, 105, 106, 108, 109, 117, 127, 132, 133, 135, 136, 149, 153–159, 161–163, 165, 166
  primary, xx, 19, 20, 24, 39, 99, 108, 122, 161, 164
  private, 14, 18–29, 32, 36, 42, 58, 60, 77, 79, 90, 102, 119, 134, 154–156, 161
Protestant, 21, 33, 41
public, xiv–xvi, xviii, xxii, 14, 21, 21, 22, 24–26, 28, 30, 31, 33–35, 37, 41, 42, 61, 91, 100, 102, 105, 119, 127, 128, 132–134, 148, 149, 156, 159–162
Republican, xvi, xviii, 130

secondary, xx, 20, 24, 25, 27, 28, 34, 43, 71, 92, 133, 134, 162, 164
Secular, xiv, xv, xx, 5, 9, 19, 20, 26, 27, 32, 33, 35, 64, 77, 103, 109, 117, 128, 131, 139
  education, 20
Secularism, xi–xv, 41, 156, 161. *See also* Laïcité
  breach, 12
Segregation, 6, 42, 44, 88, 129, 160
Seine-St-Denis, xix, xx, 76, 80, 87, 96, 117–121
Separation, xviii, 12, 20, 22, 28, 36, 121, 135
  Church and State, xviii, 20, 22, 28
Social class, 25, 43, 125, 126
State, xvi, 6, 11–13, 18–25, 27, 30, 34, 38, 40, 57, 59, 68, 82–84, 86, 90, 97, 101, 106, 109, 115, 119, 134, 154–156, 161, 163
  policies, 6
Subsidies, xv, xviii, 21, 22, 24, 25, 68. *See also* Contract

T
Teacher, xx, 10, 13, 14, 18–20, 22–24, 29, 36, 39–41, 43–45, 55, 57, 59–63, 65, 68–72, 78, 79, 82, 86, 91–93, 96, 100, 102, 105, 110–112, 114, 116, 118, 125, 127, 129–131, 133–149, 155–157, 159, 161
  compensation, 24
  status, 4, 10, 24–26, 96
  training, 25, 39, 40, 57, 67, 72, 114, 161, 166

Terrorism/terrorist, xiii, 3, 60, 83, 129, 140, 142
Textbook, 33, 69, 129, 130, 134–136, 139
Turkish, 70, 164, 168
Tutoring, xx, 76, 77, 113, 114, 120, 121, 156

U
Underprivileged, 11, 30, 42, 44, 101, 125, 126
Union Européenne pour l'Enseignement privé Musulman (UEPM), 31, 162, 164, 165
Universalism, xviii, 5, 7, 12
UOIF, xv, 15, 61, 62, 66, 72, 93, 122, 162, 163, 165

V
Veil, xiv, xv, 6, 64, 68, 79, 132, 161. *See also* Headscarf
Visibility/visible, 4, 6, 7, 10, 15, 115, 118, 129

W
West, xiii, xvi, 3, 21, 138, 153, 158
Withdrawal/*repli*, 5, 6, 35, 37

Z
Zapping, 28, 29
Zitouni, Soufiane, 59, 61, 62, 72, 157

Printed in the United States
By Bookmasters